Cambridge Elements ≡

Elements in Publishing and Book Culture
edited by
Samantha Rayner
University College London
Leah Tether
University of Bristol

THE HROSWITHA CLUB AND THE IMPACT OF WOMEN BOOK COLLECTORS

Kate Ozment
California State Polytechnic University, Pomona

CAMBRIDGE
UNIVERSITY PRESS

Shaftesbury Road, Cambridge CB2 8EA, United Kingdom

One Liberty Plaza, 20th Floor, New York, NY 10006, USA

477 Williamstown Road, Port Melbourne, VIC 3207, Australia

314–321, 3rd Floor, Plot 3, Splendor Forum, Jasola District Centre,
New Delhi – 110025, India

103 Penang Road, #05–06/07, Visioncrest Commercial, Singapore 238467

Cambridge University Press is part of Cambridge University Press & Assessment,
a department of the University of Cambridge.

We share the University's mission to contribute to society through the pursuit of
education, learning and research at the highest international levels of excellence.

www.cambridge.org
Information on this title: www.cambridge.org/9781009257206

DOI: 10.1017/9781009257183

First published 2023

A catalogue record for this publication is available from the British Library.

ISBN 978-1-009-25720-6 Paperback
ISSN 2514-8524 (online)
ISSN 2514-8516 (print)

The Hroswitha Club and the Impact of Women Book Collectors

Elements in Publishing and Book Culture

DOI: 10.1017/9781009257183

First published online: April 2023

Kate Ozment

California State Polytechnic University, Pomona

Author for correspondence: Kate Ozment, keozment@cpp.edu

ABSTRACT: The Hroswitha Club was a group of women book collectors who met from 1944 to 2004 in the Eastern United States. Despite the fame of individual members like Henrietta Bartlett or Mary Hyde Eccles, there is no sustained study of the Club's work and legacy. This Element makes this history broadly accessible and focuses on how members shared knowledge and expertise and provided a space for legitimacy and self-growth in a period where women's access to formal education and academic institutions was limited. By making this network visible through a study of archival records, library catalogs, and pamphlets, this project positions the Club as a case study for a more thorough examination of the ways that intersectional identities can make visible or obscure whose intellect, money, and resources have shaped the study of rare books in the United States.

KEYWORDS: women book collectors, feminist studies, book history and bibliography, the Hroswitha Club, the Grolier Club

ISBNs: 9781009257206 (PB), 9781009257183 (OC)
ISSNs: 2514-8524 (online), 2514-8516 (print)

Contents

Introduction: The Hroswitha Club and Historical Significance

This project began in March 2019 when a Wikipedia editor marked the Hroswitha Club page for deletion because the group was not significant enough. I was just getting interested in the topic, as an extension of a project on women bibliographers, and was excited by how many prominent names were involved in the Hroswitha Club. The page was marked for deletion during Women's History Month, of all times, which fed into an annoyance that prompted me to spend a week in New York in the Grolier Club library, overseen by the Club's librarian Meghan Constantinou. The trip was self-financed, based on a gut feeling that there was more here worth exploring and that the Hroswitha Club's dismissal as "not significant" was likely a reaction in a long line of bookish misogyny I had come to know well. That feeling was correct, and this Element is the result.

The Hroswitha Club was a private club that met from 1944 to 2004, and membership included around 100 collectors, librarians, and bibliographers whose collections and labor have contributed to more than seventy-five institutions, including Harvard's Houghton Library, Princeton's Firestone Library, Carnegie Mellon's Hunt Library, and the Morgan Library & Museum. Despite this, institutions with collections from these women may be surprised to learn of their connection to the Hroswitha Club. It was common for a private women's social club of this era to prefer intimate rather than public attention, and members were rarely named as a Hroswithian in the articles they did appear in. These articles were almost exclusively about socially notable events – births, deaths, marriages, divorces, and occasionally philanthropic work – and obituaries defaulted to well-known organizations like the Garden Club of America. This relative silence is notable when compared to the Grolier Club, a men-only bibliophile club until 1976, and similar organizations that had exhibitions, journals, and numerous newspaper features. Deceased men from these clubs are usually named as such in obituaries. Arguments about the Hroswitha Club's "significance," then, is a gendered thing, tangled in rules of feminine propriety and assumptions about what makes something worthy of discussion, as women's history so often is.

This Element argues that the Hroswitha Club is the most significant group of women book collectors in US history. This is a novel argument only because of the idiosyncrasies of women's history in general and women and rare books in particular. The work of this Element is twofold. First, it engages in recovery work that details who the Hroswitha Club was and examines how the group impacted the study of rare books and artifacts in the United States. By working with the Hroswitha Club archives at the Grolier Club along with members' papers at Brown, Princeton, Harvard, and Yale, this Element constructs the first list of members that is printed outside the organization, uses women's full names rather than married honorifics, and tracks where their collections were deposited. The narrative that follows largely relies on undigitized documentary records, which consist of meeting minutes and directories; ephemera and material traces of meetings such as formal invitations; research conducted for the club's publications; and to a lesser extent the Hroswitha Club library. Much of this narrative will be through the members' own words, especially those of the recording secretaries: Bertha Slade, Anne Haight, Katharine Bull, Phyllis Gordan, Julia Wightman, and Chantal Hodges.

Secondly, this Element uses a feminist lens to examine how gender norms influenced members' engagement with the masculinized world of rare books. While only some of these women would have or did identify as feminist, their self-determined expectations as collectors resisted gender norms for middle- and upper-class women who were to be only wives and mothers. To consider their stories and the politics of book collecting and philanthropy, I rely on feminist writing that positions gender as one axis of identity enmeshed with race, sexuality, and class. My understanding of gender as embedded within intersecting axes of power rather than a single-axis framework pulls from the work of Black feminists, particularly the Combahee River Collective's *identity politics*, Audre Lorde's *mythical norm*, and Kimberlé Crenshaw's *intersectionality*.[1] Inspired by this work, I think about the act of collecting physical books as reflective of cultural beliefs about power structures related to

---

[1] I especially pull from theory by Black, Indigenous, and Women of Color in the United States from the 1970s to now for this understanding. See Lorde, and Taylor, and Crenshaw.

identity. As books change hands, value is assigned and reassigned based on the cultural and economic capital these objects command. Cultural capital is reflective of social power structures: what price something commands and who is willing to buy it are complicated value judgments easily swayed by gendered, sexualized, and racialized power dynamics. Feminist analysis can explain some of politics of this circuit of exchange along with giving language for the casual neglecting or forgetting of women's collecting as meaningful labor in the process.

Through these dual interests, this Element reveals that in a period where women's formal education and participation in historical and cultural institutions were limited, the women of the Hroswitha Club created pathways for their own enrichment, scholarship, and fellowship. Their network repositions figures like Belle da Costa Greene, Margaret Stillwell, and Henrietta C. Bartlett as part of a community rather than gendered exceptions to the cis-male-focused norm in rare books. It links previously disparate records of collection donations and sales and allows us to see how much this largely untracked group has shaped the study of rare books and artifacts at more than seventy-five institutions in the United States and Great Britain. It is high time we told their stories.

1 "Very Serious and Very Excellent": Who Were the Hroswithians?

In April 1944, with World War II raging as a backdrop, eight women met for lunch at the Cosmopolitan Club in Manhattan: Anne Lyon Haight, Henrietta Collins Bartlett, Mabel Choate, Sarah Gildersleeve Fife, Ruth Shepard Granniss, Belle da Costa Greene, Rachel McMasters Miller Hunt, and Eleanor Cross Marquand. They were some of the most distinguished women collectors, librarians, bibliographers, and scholars on the East Coast.

Haight was a world traveler who was on the first Pan Am clipper passenger flights across the Atlantic and to South America and was a member of the Society of Women Geographers; she collected examples of early printing and women printers and published in venues such as *Bookmaking on the Distaff Side* (1937). Choate owned two estates in Massachusetts – Naumkeag and the Mission House – and dedicated her time to their renovation and preservation, with particular emphasis on botany and gardens. Fife collected books on gardens, flora, and fauna and was heavily involved in the Garden Club of America, the Horticultural Society of New York, and the New York Botanical Gardens, the last of which has a prize named in her honor. Hunt was a talented bookbinder and had a substantial library of botanicals, the finest of which were described by Jane Quinby in the *Hunt Catalogue*; her library and endowment became the Hunt Institute for Botanical Documentation at Carnegie Mellon. Marquand collected botany and religious imagery, particularly focusing on iconography of flowers and trees, for which she was granted an honorary degree from Princeton. Greene was director of the Morgan Library & Museum and was an authority on incunables and medieval manuscripts; her work substantially reshaped the Morgan from its roots as a private library into a research institution.[2] Granniss was retired from a forty-year career as the Grolier Club's librarian, and she was an active contributor to academic journals and coordinated numerous exhibits at the Grolier Club.[3] Bartlett

---

[2] Morgan Library & Museum, "Belle Da Costa Greene."

[3] Abraham, "Ruth Shepard Granniss."

cataloged Beverly Chew's library and was a legendary bibliographer of Shakespeare's works, largely through her work at Yale, whose collations are still in use.[4]

These women were the founding members of the Hroswitha Club, and they represented a typical split in the club's interests and backgrounds. Haight, Choate, Fife, Hunt, and Marquand were avocational collectors without traditional employment in these fields, and they used their collections to educate themselves and carve out a role in the creation of academic knowledge. Greene, Granniss, and Bartlett were vocational bibliophiles with professional expertise and either formal educational training or that gained through an apprenticeship model. Although these eight women came from different backgrounds, ranging from middle-class lives to incredible wealth, they all shared a love of books and an interest in sharing their expertise through informal education.

They started the Hroswitha Club because an existing organization would not do – none fit the brief. Women's clubs were popular in this period, a holdover from the women's club movement near the beginning of the twentieth century, but most focused on reading books rather than collecting them.[5] And in turn, book collector clubs would not admit women. Many of the original avocational members were wives of the Grolier Club members, and they were only conditionally allowed to engage in the Club's activities. They could attend "Lady's Days" and teas or come to events by invitation, but they could not be members or attend the Club's functions and use its library at will. Importantly, single women like Greene and Bartlett, no matter their expertise or interests, could not attend events or trips as wives could. Fife positioned the new Hroswitha Club as the women's alternative to the Grolier Club, sometimes informally referred to as "the female Grolier." When she wrote to new members to invite them to join, she explained that the goal of the Hroswitha Club would be "to exchange ideas and cultivate in any way possible our interest in and love of books."[6] Taking a nod from the Grolier Club's model, the Hroswitha Club

---

[4] Lesser and Houghton, "Recovering Henrietta Bartlett."

[5] For more on women's clubs, see Hendricks, Scheil, and Long.

[6] Fife, "Letter to Mrs. Dickey, n.p.

was named after a notable literary figure – Hrosvitha of Gandersheim, a woman playwright. Indicative of the club's commitment to scholarly discourse, this decision was made over the course of a year with some debate about Hrosvitha's authenticity led by Greene, one of the club's medievalists.

Rather than challenging the single-sex social norm and pushing the Grolier Club to allow women, they created their own homosocial space where their work would be valued, and they could learn from one another when other institutions would not have them. They quickly found like-minded colleagues. Eight members grew to thirty, then forty, and that number was maintained to the 1990s. Notable members include Margaret Bingham Stillwell, a bibliographer who has the honor of being an eponymous reference for incunables; Anne Seddon Kinsolving Brown, who collected military books and objects, now at Brown University; Mary Hyde Eccles, whose expansive collection of Samuel Johnson is at the Houghton Library and her equally impressive one of Oscar Wilde is at the British Library; Miriam Young Holden, a feminist activist whose library on women's history is at Princeton; Phyllis Goodhart Gordan, a founding member of the Renaissance Society of America; and Mabel Zahn, a familiar figure at Sessler's bookstore in Philadelphia.

While their origins were in exclusion from the Grolier Club and the two groups always had friendly relations, few Hroswithians felt that a characterization of the Hroswitha Club as the "female Grolier" was sufficient in the long term; they largely thought of themselves on their own terms. Illustratively, when Haight was the club's president in 1957, she was interviewed about their activities: "The Club is an organization of women book collectors, very serious and very excellent ones" she told *The New Yorker*, firmly, in the only mainstream periodical piece on the club.[7] Haight's sentiments seem to be generally shared by other members, and the group positioned themselves as erudite women with serious book collections who had a good deal to teach one another from their libraries, their study of these collections, and their hunt for new objects. As part of their activities, members would frequently give lectures and display their

[7] *The New Yorker*, "Hroswithians," p. 18.

collections, which included incunables, herbals and botany, American first editions, British classics, children's literature, regional histories, prints and illustrations, and themed collection on sports, fauna like bees and pigs, or iconography. These activities seem to have been enriching and personally quite important for a core group of the members, who used meetings and field excursions as public engagement with a thriving culture of rare books and literature.

But to get a fuller picture of who was in the Hroswitha Club, I will step back from its more famous members to take stock of the group as a whole. Prior to this Element, a complete membership list has not been generally available. The list in the appendix was compiled by comparing printed membership lists from 1944 to 1994, which yielded 102 members. There are more who joined between 1994 and 2004 whose names can be found in the archive, such as Sarah Peters, but the records are less consistent, and I have elected to limit my survey to the first fifty years as a starting point. Membership lists were formal documents, and thus recorded all married women's names as "Mrs. Husband Lastname," and it took a significant amount of time to track down the women's familiar and family names. The bulk of this effort was completed with Kelly Wong, an undergraduate research assistant, without whom this invaluable recovery work would not be possible.[8] We are still unsure of given names for a few of the members or if collections were sold or given to children, as records indicate.

---

[8] See Wong, "Collector's Role" for her take on this project. We used a combination of the meeting minutes, general search engines, genealogy databases, and periodicals to locate women's given names. Names were usually found in census documents and marriage, divorce, and death notices in newspapers. The particularly difficult names were located with help from the rare book community, including the Grolier Club librarian Meghan Constantinou, the Grolier Club members, those who answered queries on SHARP-L and the Ex-Libris listservs, and those who follow me on Twitter. In particular, we would like to thank Emily Spunaugle, Alan Kabat, Jeremy Dibbell, Elizabeth DeBold, Elizabeth Denlinger, William M. Klimon, Terry Belanger, Joseph L. Felcone, Ashley Cataldo, and Elizabeth Carroll-Horrocks. Blogs from Emiko Hastings and Kurt Zimmerman were also valuable resources.

While it is difficult to say something concrete about more than 100 women whose lives intersected over a fifty-year period, there are some trends in the membership that make visible the dynamics of what kind of woman was included in this group of women book collectors. The most stable category is gender – all members identified as women, as far as the documents as my disposal can say. Their participation in the social norms of womanhood was drawn in narrow terms at the surface level. The majority were born in the United States, married people who identified as men, and had children. Those who went to college and married tended to shift their vocation from academic or artistic pursuits toward homemaking and child-rearing. A few of the women divorced, which became less taboo as time passed, and some remarried.

In other ways, Hroswithians resisted gendered norms for middle- and upper-class women of this period. Deirdre Howard Pirie was a four-in-hand carriage driver who competed at an international level. In a memoir posted to Facebook, the West Newbury Riding Club wrote that she "would mow fields, plant gardens, blow snow, gallop racehorses, repair broken tack and blankets. When her carriages broke, over and over in competition, she enrolled herself and members of her staff in welding lessons, so she would know a good weld from bad and prevent delays in training her horses."[9] Other women never married or remained childless. The three initial honorary members were unmarried: Greene, Bartlett, and Granniss. Many of the single women had careers, likely a necessity to support themselves, but certainly it could have been by choice because they enjoyed their careers and did not want to give them up for marriage and children, as married women like Violetta White Delafield or Rachel Hunt experienced.[10] A persistent contingent of unmarried professionals was joined by single women with financial independence: Julia Parker Wightman, Alice Brayton, and Clara Sargent Peck, among others. These

---

[9] West Newbury Riding Driving Club, n.p.

[10] Delafield's mycology work largely ceased when she married, and Hunt's book-binding became much more sparing when she had children. A frequent trend in accounts of these women's lives is that childrearing and families had set expectations that would come before collecting or related activities.

women were wealthy enough, and in control of their wealth, that they could pursue collecting and bibliophilia as a passion rather than a professional vocation.

All these women could have remained unmarried because they simply did not enjoy the company of men or the heteronormative expectations of marriage. There are no "out" lesbians, transgender people, or asexual or bisexual women that I could find through additional research, but Bartlett and Granniss were certainly intimate friends and Eve Houghton's research may uncover additional dynamics to their relationship.[11] Marriage would have been a social given for many regardless of orientation or preferences, and the formal nature of club records and academic publications renders private lives opaque. As much as I can glean through formal texts, some of these women certainly lived queer lives in that they undermined the heterosexual norm by remaining unmarried and centering personal fulfillment over procreation.[12] Future research could explore more of this approach to individual collectors or the broader homosocial relationships of the club.[13]

Most of the women were white. The only member I have identified as otherwise is Greene, who was Black and passed as Portuguese to avoid stigma in New York social circles,[14] but biographical research may reveal more variation as there was certainly an impetus to pass as normatively white in the circles these women moved in. Whiteness is always being legislated and reformed, and a few of the women would have faced other social and political challenges due to ethnicity and nationality as different groups are "allowed" to be white or excluded based on arbitrary designations.[15] At least one member was Jewish, Edith Goodkind

[11] Houghton, "Henrietta Bartlett and the 1916 Census of Shakespeare Quartos," n.p.

[12] This positioning pulls from Rich's classic essay on compulsory heterosexuality.

[13] For the study of homosociality, see Sedgwick (1985).

[14] Ardizzone, *An Illuminated Life*.

[15] The arbitrariness of whiteness is a central tenant of critical race studies in general, and whiteness studies in particular. For more on legislating whiteness, see Hughey and Pollak.

Rosenwald, and others were immigrants, such as Lola Szladits and Frances Kennedy Black.

Class had variation. Early membership was largely avocational bibliographers and collectors. They self-described as amateurs with their primary vocation as raising children and housekeeping. These women seem to have been predominately middle and upper class, with some variation toward more modest means and some who were incredibly wealthy. Many of the library workers were closer to middle class, and it is likely by design that honorary members (who were working professionals) did not pay dues and were frequently treated to events. Many club members would have had domestic workers in the home, though this is only slightingly mentioned in the formal meeting minutes or biographies. In 1963, it is noted that "Mrs. [Gertrude] Fay had just imported a maid from Germany named Hroswitha."[16] Members were able to take trains and the occasional plane when strikes and weather permitted, and RSVP cards show that chauffeured cars and limos were sent around New York City to pick up guests for meetings in the 1940s and 1950s. Hosts tended to underwrite these events, and as the following sections will detail, the wealthier hosts threw rather lavish parties. Judging from these factors in conversation with purchasing power, it is safe to say most of the women would have been financially comfortable and a majority were well-off.

Class and wealth are important indicators about a collector's abilities to collect and how they might garner access to institutions and information that allow them to gain subject-matter expertise. Mary Hyde Eccles commented on the intersection of gender and collecting in her 1990 talk at the Grolier Club, where she was one of the first two women members. Virginia Woolf identified that women needed "a room of one's own" and £500 a year to be a writer, and Eccles resonantly argued that women collectors needed time, money, and freedom.[17] Eccles is a particularly good example of this happy intersection. She and her first husband Donald Hyde traveled the world in search of books, including multiple trips to Japan for a collection that was later sold to benefit the Morgan Library. She married David Eccles,

---

[16] Wightman, "Minutes of the Hroswitha Club," February 1963, n.p.

[17] Quoted in Morris, "Mary Hyde and the Unending Pursuit."

also a notable bibliophile, after Donald's passing. The Hydes were comfortable, with early investments in General Electric and American Airlines supporting their lifestyles, and they frequently provided monetary donations to support the libraries in their orbit, such as helping Yale buy a copy of the Bay Psalms book in 1947.[18] Mary Hyde was an amateur scholar only in the sense that she was not formally employed by a university to complete her scholarship. She was educated at Vassar and Columbia with a focus on the Renaissance before her interests shifted to the 1700s. She was on editorial boards for major projects, including the Eighteenth-Century Short Title Catalogue and the Samuel Johnson papers, the latter of which was a major interest as a collector and scholar. Her papers at the Houghton join an impressive collection of Johnson and his circle that she accumulated Donald Hyde, and in them we glean that she also had enough time and freedom to do her work. Her calendars demonstrate how she worked through intense writing projects: she was routine and meticulous with appointments stacked on a few days a week and research the rest. Her correspondence has many examples of her turning down more work so she could finish the project in front of her, a remarkable ability for an academic. Even when she was busy, on her calendars Saturdays were for James Boswell, locked in the circular office at Two River Farm surrounded by books and impeccably dressed in strings of pearls.[19]

Along with Eccles, some Hroswithians were fortunate enough to have time, money, and freedom in differing degrees; how much freedom a wife and mother in the 1950s had is debatable, but the Hroswithians seemed to clearly carve out space for their activities. A few had them in enough abundance to collect in ways that earned notice, named collections, and sometimes named buildings. These were on the wealthier side, and they feature a cast of well-known archetypes from the Gilded Age. They were the daughters and wives of quite a few bank executives, directors of department stores, oil and steel barons, railroad administrators, and

---

[18] President and Fellows of Yale University, Letter to Mr. and Mrs. Donald Hyde, 1947. The book is in the Beinecke Rare Book and Manuscript Library, call number MLm405 640b.

[19] As pictured in an Untitled Photograph, 1967, in her papers at the Houghton.

plantation owners. Some could trace their family heritages to original colonists from Europe and relied on generational wealth. Class, wealth, their associated connections, and the promise of a donation or collection also opened quite a few doors for the Hroswithians. In an interview, former club president Susanna Borghese emphasized that much of the early membership would rely on their philanthropic ties to garner access to libraries that were limited to male students and researchers.

Because most institutions were limited to men at the beginning of the Hroswitha Club's tenure, education for its members varied widely. In the early years, some members came to the club with training from attending prestigious single-sex schools, like the Brearley School and St. Timothy's in Maryland, and universities like Bryn Mawr, Barnard College, and the other "Seven Sisters," East Coast institutions that catered to a selective female student body with a liberal arts education. Some women used university to pursue interests before marrying, a social norm that Betty Friedan lamented in *The Feminine Mystique*. Others in the Hroswitha Club pursued education to support themselves, generally as librarians, which was a field that was friendly (if not equitable) toward women workers.[20] In later years, librarians would be joined by curators and professors with doctorates. Some Hroswithians understood formal education past grade school and perhaps high school as superfluous. For example, Wightman "was entirely dependent on servants, did not go to college, and lived with her much-loved parents until their death."[21] As Elizabeth Denlinger argues, if Wightman, an heiress, did not spell particularly well, it did not really matter. Others were socialized into not attending or could have been pressured by traditional family members who found it eccentric or uncomfortably progressive. If they did not have an independent fortune, financial dependence would have required deference to parental or spousal, and largely masculine, authority.

Membership was built on professional, social, and familial networks, since existing members nominated new ones. The papers of the professional members help us map these ties. In her capacity as a bibliographer and book

---

[20] See Taylor and Coleman, Jr.   [21] Denlinger, "Julia Parker Wightman," p. 2.

collector, Bartlett wrote to Granniss, Greene, Eccles, Dorothy Miner, and other Hroswithians' working husbands, like Gilbert Troxell. When Granniss was celebrated for thirty years as the Grolier Club librarian in 1935, it was Bartlett who toasted her, praising her diplomacy, "kindness, knowledge, and patience" as she detailed how they worked together to give women scholars greater access to the library for research.[22] Granniss and Bartlett were lifelong friends who published a typography book together,[23] but there are few of the letters between them in Bartlett's papers. Eve Houghton hypothesizes that a lack of textual traces indicates a greater intimacy: they did not often write as they were physically together (they lived together for eighteen years) or they did not save their letters because they did not want public viewing of their correspondence.[24] Members knew each other from the Cosmopolitan and Colony Clubs or the Garden Club of America – gardening and botany are particularly strong collecting emphases for early members in particular. Family ties are also traceable: there were three Spragues simultaneously in the 1950s; Emily English and Sarah Fife were sisters, Clelia and Violetta Delafield were sisters-in-law; and Mary Massey was Frances Massey's mother.

This overview of the membership makes some dynamics visible. Members cannot be considered as a monolithic group due to their pointed differences in education, class, and background. Throughout this narrative is an interplay of privilege that opens doors and discrimination and closes them a few hours later. Most were socialized into roles as wives and mothers regardless of if it best fit their personalities or goals, but they did have some level of choice and agency, which was different from multiply marginalized women for whom education and higher social status was a much more difficult journey.[25] This understanding of the members will ground my analysis of the activities, projects, and legacy of these women collectors in particular and the study of rare books more broadly in the following sections.

---

[22] Bartlett, "Ruth Granniss Celebration Speech." Bartlett's other correspondence with Grolier includes requests to admit women researchers.

[23] Bartlett and Granniss's collaboration was A Garland of Poppies (1905).

[24] Houghton, "Henrietta Bartlett and the 1916 Census of Shakespeare Quartos," n. p. and Houghton, Eve 2022. pers. comm.

[25] hooks, *Feminist Theory from Margin to Center*.

2 "Land of Bibliophilia": Women and Book Collecting

Beyond the differences in their backgrounds and interests, the unifying motivation that united this disparate group of women is a love of collecting and book collecting specifically. This interest troubled social norms for women of this period, as it involved "hunting" for objects as a competition rather than for sentimental reasons. Secondly, these women largely focused on books, objects with a particular masculinized history due to their association with academic study, and rare books were even more taboo because of the additional monetary and cultural value attached to them. This section will explicate both dynamics and the complex and gendered world that the Hroswitha Club navigated before detailing what they collected.

Susan M. Pearce defines collecting as "the gathering together and setting aside of selected objects."[26] When we study collecting, we "tease out an understanding of how communities develop strategies which enable them to bring together the accumulating possibilities of objects and other social structures . . . in order to maintain the social pattern and project it out into the future.[27]" Collections are positioned in this understanding as not simply accumulating objects themselves, but the "possibilities" of objects within communities centered on a common goal. When a group of collectors shares a mutual possibility, they can develop strategies for achieving it together.

Like literature, bibliography, and history, the study of collecting has been characterized by a dearth of women. However, Tom Stammers observes that changes in the field have challenged the belief that there were no women collectors. He argues that as "the focus has shifted from laudatory accounts of the lives and taste of great men," a consequence is "the definition of what counts as a collection has also expanded dramatically."[28] This expansion includes sentimental objects rather than ones deemed to have monetary value, and thus a history emerges not only

---

[26] Pearce, *On Collecting*, p. 3. [27] Pearce, *On Collecting*, p. 28.

[28] Stammers, "Women Collectors and Cultural Philanthropy," n.p.

of women art collectors but also of buttons, flowers, postcards, furnishings, dresses, and jewelry collectors.[29] Just as men ordered objects around them for various sentimental, economic, social, and political reasons, "female collectors, whatever their rank in society, chose to collect and what to collect; they chose how and where to present the collection; they also decided if to preserve and when to dispose of objects, thereby taking on a curatorial role."[30]

Women taking on active roles is an increasingly common way to interpret collecting habits, and it characterizes most of the women in the Hroswitha Club. Dianne Sachko Macleod argues that "collecting not only contributed to [women's] self-esteem but also induced a great many of them to expand their spatial maps by enticing them out of the home, into the thriving American cultural scene."[31] It is easy to draw a parallel from Macleod's elite women art collectors and the book collectors who made up the Hroswitha Club. While some of them like Haight were world travelers, for others the Club would have been a spatial expansion with access to institutions otherwise limited. The Hroswitha Club, like other organizations in the women's club movement, could serve as a legitimizing function for these women's lives and work. As their obituaries detail, Hroswithians were heavily involved in these clubs and volunteered with social and cultural institutions from libraries to hospitals, schools, historical societies, museums, and heritage groups. Newspaper photos depict them handing out books to children and the sick.[32]

Book collecting has characteristics that differentiate it from other forms of collecting, and some of these characteristics are gendered. For one thing, book collectors tend to believe they are the best sort of collectors and have written numerous volumes about the practice and their collections.[33] The desire to collect books is frequently characterized as an ailment or disease of *bibliomania*, the "gentle madness."[34] Book collectors are enamored with

---

[29] Gelber, *Hobbies*.

[30] Bracken, Gáldy, and Turpin, *Women Patrons and Collectors*, p. xvi.

[31] Macleod, *Enchanted Lives*, p. 17. [32] As an example, see Teltsch.

[33] For a useful survey of literature on book collecting, see Tanselle.

[34] See Basbanes.

what Jack Matthews calls a "symbolically intensified object" because while other objects can be aesthetically beautiful, "Books possess individual personalities; they possess interiors much like the interiors of human beings."[35] The symbolism of these objects is intensified by books' connection to public presentation of information and academic knowledge, which are masculinized spaces in the Anglo-American world. Consequently, women's involvement in this space can be fraught. This tension is perhaps epitomized by William Blades' *The Enemies of Books* (1888), which characterizes women with dusters as an invading "enemy" of books, alongside servants, children, vermin, dust, fire, water, and neglect. Books are for serious study, inevitably only in men's libraries and academic spaces. Blades' vision of a sanitized library where only grown, educated, upper-class men can correctly care for books was published during the Victorian period when the rise of public libraries and women librarians threatened the homosocial masculinity signified by books, including their collection and study of the knowledge they contained. The members of the Hroswitha Club would have been described as invading women by Blades, but in reality they had their own libraries and were experts on the care and study of their books. Despite Blades' argument, women have been book collectors as long as there have been books, which Emiko Hastings, Melanie Bigold, A. S. W. Rosenbach, and Heléna Tóth have showed in examples spanning centuries.

The woman book collector has yet to have a book about her, as Hastings observes, and thus it is not surprising that relatively little is known about a specific women book collectors club in New York.[36] Women collectors often understood themselves as singular figures, sometimes with pleasure but more often with dismay. In her project on women bibliophiles, Hastings has gathered extracts from women reflecting on their identity as collectors.[37] In one illustrative example from a 1933 *Book Collector* article, Genevieve B. Earle writes: "Ever since, I've had an exciting time with books, bookshops, auction sales, etc., but never once have I seen or heard of a woman book-collector. Where do women book-collectors keep themselves? Have they no clubs, no haunts, no

---

[35] Matthews, *Collecting Rare Books*, p. 14.

[36] Hastings, "Mighty Women Book Hunters."

[37] Hastings, "Women Collectors in Their Own Words."

rendez-vous? The Land of Bibliophilia must be the Garden of Eden with the Adams in complete possession of all their ribs."[38]

Earle's longing for an Eve in the "Land of Bibliophilia" is certainly evocative for this history of a women's book collecting club that started a decade after the article was published. There was a sense that women collectors were isolated exceptions, and they had no space to gather and share their collections to fight such a perception.

The necessity of such a space was filled by the Hroswitha Club, and its members collected widely. To get a broad look at their interests, I completed a survey using members' self-identified collecting foci in membership lists.[39] These interests are replicated in the appendix. Table 1 lays out an overview of the collectors' interests by genre.

Most of the club was interested in collecting codices and manuscripts. Within this, the biggest interest was literature, which includes foci on specific authors, genres, time periods, and geographic locations. Particularly well-represented were British and American authors, especially nineteenth-century white male authors, and children's literature. Hroswithians were interested in history, which ranged from ancient to contemporary, global to hyper focused on the Hudson Valley. Most of the science and natural history collectors gathered books on botany, herbals, and illustrations of flora and fauna. Book parts and book history gesture to the librarians, bibliographers, and binders who collected based on bibliographic significance. This group includes women who collected not only for content but a particular physical trait, like an embroidered binding, a miniature book, bookplates, or books made of vellum.

---

[38] Quoted in Hastings, "Women Collectors in Their Own Words."

[39] The taxonomy for this survey was developed from seeing what would be most useful based on what is in front of me. When something seemed to fit in multiple categories, I marked it multiple times, and consequently the total will be more than the total number of collectors.

Table 1 A table representing the self-assigned collecting interests of members of the Hroswitha Club

Collection Focus	No. of Collectors
Architecture	4
Art and Artists	11
Book History (incl. incunables)	15
Book Parts (bindings, vellum, etc.)	22
History (incl. biography)	27
Literature	54
Music	2
Reference	9
Religion	5
Science and Natural History	24
Painting, Prints, and Drawings	5
Furnishings	2
Great House Restoration	3
Other Media (silver, ceramics, etc.)	9

The diversity of collection topics emphasizes the range of expertise that the group represented. A requirement of quality collecting is becoming knowledgeable on the chosen topic and its means of transmission – in this case, usually a book, painting, or household good. G. Thomas Tanselle argues that "The collector must understand something of the history of printing and publishing, must be able to analyze the physical evidence present in books, and must know how to read technical descriptions of books" and that the literature of bibliographical description is essential for collectors.[40] As a result of this reality, most of these women were art historians and bibliographers by necessity so they could understand the financial, social, and aesthetic value of their

[40] Tanselle, "Literature of Book Collecting," p. 210.

collections. Violetta White Delafield's mycology collection included her own watercolors and illustrations which allowed her to publish in academic journals; Eleanor Cross Marquand became an authority on representations of flowers and trees through her collection of botanical illustrations and herbals; Mary Preston Massey amassed "probably the best and most comprehensive collection of rare and early herbals in the United States" as a "knowledgeable and discriminating collector"; and Margaret Bell Douglas collected plant specimens and donated more than 1,500 to the herbarium of Desert Botanical Garden in Phoenix, Arizona, where she retired.[41] As another example, Henrietta Bartlett developed a knowledge of Early Modern literature and bibliography while cataloging Beverly Chew's library. She worked on a legendary *Census* of Shakespeare's works with Alfred W. Pollard, which allowed her to cultivate an informal but extensive knowledge of these books. She wrote in 1916, "Alas, I never heard of a degree and am merely a humble person who happens to know something about Shakespeare."[42] Bartlett's work with the Elizabethan Club's Shakespeare collection led to honorary membership in 1954, the first for a woman in the club's history,[43] in addition to quite a few honorary degrees and a reputation as one of the foremost bibliographers of the twentieth century. With respect to Bartlett's self-assessment, few of us would call this legacy "humble." An emphasis on self-education and subsequent sharing of information resonated with women's clubs as vehicle for personal enrichment, and it allowed women like Bartlett to have a forum where she could share this knowledge and learn from others' expertise.

In addition to passive resistance of gendered norms by being women book collectors, Hroswithians also took on forms of collecting that were

---

[41] See Slack; "Eleanor Cross Marquand Papers"; Folger Shakespeare Library; and "Margaret Bell Douglas (1880–1963)," respectively.

[42] Quoted in Houghton, "I Am Always Sorry to Antagonize Collectors."

[43] My thanks to Basie Gitlin for access to this information and more context on the club's history at Yale.

more typically associated with men. They largely bought and sold objects rather than finding them, making them, or receiving them through gifts, which is more typical of women's collecting. Steven M. Gelber explains that collecting when value is assigned to objects and money is exchanged is a "specialized performance of capitalism" that centers "hunting, desire, possession, control, and order."[44] Many volumes on book collecting characterize it as a hunt, with words like "quarry."[45] While it may not have been as typical, Hroswithians were certainly on the hunt. Enabled by disposable income, they used it to engage in transactions culturally associated with men. Even those that were focused on more traditionally feminine iconography like flowers were buying and selling their books, bidding at auctions, and dealing with bookshops and tradespeople. They circled books of interest on catalogs and sent them to one another, and an aspect of the meetings involved displaying their trophies or treasures.[46] When asked what she intends to do with her collection of miniature books, former Hroswithian and bookbinder Deborah Evetts said she is tempted to sell them to let others participate in the fun of hunting them down again.[47]

As these practices indicate, the Hroswithians were not an invading duster in a masculine oasis of the feminized domain of the home, as Blades phrased it, but actively reshaping the home itself for their collections. More than one rebuilt a structure to accommodate a library, even recreating eighteenth-century architecture for their books and antiques. Louise Elkins Sinkler had Sir Henry St. John's library, where Alexander Pope is said to have written *Essay on Man*, shipped from England and rebuilt as part of Guilford Estate, and Marjorie Wiggin Prescott rebuilt her library to avoid fire hazards and protect her books.[48]

As these two examples indicate, many Hroswithians certainly spent a good deal of money caring for their books and bookish interests. But, interestingly, it does not seem that many Hroswithians considered their

---

[44] Gelber, *Hobbies*, p. 102.

[45] As two examples, Stewart and Winterich and Randall. Rosenbach likens it to hunting and a sport, which he importantly includes women in.

[46] Haight, *The New Yorker*, n.p. [47] Evetts, Deborah 2022, pers. comm.

[48] Prescott, *Stray Thoughts*, p. 4–5.

books to be an investment that they hoped to financially profit from, which did motivate some collectors. Jack Matthews notes that "rare books *can* be collected realistically for investment purposes" but is careful to ascribe this motivator as second to what should always be first: a "fervent love of books."[49] Matthews is joined by both Robert A. Wilson and Prescott in this distinction. Wilson defined a collector's experience as separate from the dealer or investor in the following way: "If the acquisition of a rare, long-sought-after book gives you pleasure, a glow, a lift, just because you finally own it, with little or no thought that you may be able to sell it at a profit, then you are undoubtedly a collector."[50] Prescott agreed with this sentiment in her memoir *Stray Thoughts of a Book-Collector,* where she argues that hoping books would make you rich is "speculating" rather than collecting. She observes, "Understanding the money value of books is like knowing the price of prints, paintings, silver, furniture; one must have an honest knowledge of the subject. A real book-collector is a book-lover."[51] All three points of view emphasize that there is an intimacy between collector and object that collectors find necessary for there to be any real value to what one buys.

As an aside, Prescott's collection is one of the only Hroswithians' books that were publicly sold as a lot, and thus has an available record of how much it was worth – what her "honest knowledge of the subject" amounted to in capitalist terms. Prescott was a lifelong collector of books and antiques from a family of collectors, and in 1981, her family's collection sold through Christie's for $1.3 million, including a manuscript of Oscar Wilde's *The Importance of Being Earnest* that went for $90,000.[52] While Prescott is one of the only Hroswithians that I have located who articulated in print a point of view on finances, most of the women seem to be collectors who did intentionally engage in an intimacy with their books, though it is not easy nor necessary to fully differentiate between a collector and a dealer. Mabel Zahn was a collector by passion and dealer by trade, and some of the other collections were sold at least in part.

---

[49] Matthews, *Collecting Rare Books*, p. 11. Emphasis in original.
[50] Wilson, *Modern Book Collecting*, p. 4.   [51] Prescott, *Stray Thoughts*, p. 12.
[52] Phipps, "Prescott Collection," p. 12.

While finances are a muddier aspect of this history, Hroswithians' intimacy with books certainly functioned as a mechanism of prestige and validation that could develop through the fellowship of the club. It seems their interests laid in the familiar territory of financially stable women and the wealthy: philanthropy and social heritage projects.[53] Philanthropist Hroswithians who donated money and their collections are the most well-known because big-ticket philanthropy tends to come with press releases, named collections, endowed awards, and occasionally a building. Libraries and cultural institutions courted these women for their patronage: as the next section details, at one meeting it seems most of the Princeton Library faculty, staff, and administrators met visiting Hroswithians and put on a special exhibition for them with a printed keepsake. This group of well-known Hroswithian benefactors includes Mary Hyde Eccles, Miriam Young Holden, Rachel Miller Hunt, Mildred Barnes Bliss, Janet Camp Troxell, Lillian Gary Taylor, Frances Milliken Hooper, Clara Sargent Peck, and Anne Burr Auchincloss Lewis. They represent collections at the Houghton and British Libraries, the Holden Collection at Princeton, the Hunt Library at Carnegie Mellon, Dumbarton Oaks, the Troxell Collection at Princeton, the Taylor Family Collection at the University of Virginia, collections of Hooper's works and papers at Smith College and the University of Chicago, the Clara S. Peck collection at the Corning Museum of Glass and Rockwell Museum, and the Lewis Walpole Library at Yale, respectively. They are peers to collectors whose endowments and collections have supported and created the Huntington, Folger Shakespeare, Newberry, and Clark libraries.

The notion of a donation or endowment coupled with personal ties and relationships allowed Hroswithians greater access to these institutions, and it is difficult to downplay the importance of this dynamic in characterizing the club's mechanisms. While they may not have understood these as investments they hoped to personally recoup from (though there are financial benefits to philanthropic donations in the United States), they were able to leverage wealth and other markers of privilege to acquire significance and prestige that was generally denied women. Princeton

[53] My thanks to Rebecca More for identifying this latter trend for me.

would not have admitted Eleanor Marquand, Miriam Holden, or Janet Troxell as students or hired them as teachers, but they could influence the institution through notable and impressive collections. Holden was particularly motivated to donate her collection to Princeton because the first coeds were admitted in degree-granting programs in 1969, and she believed that women needed books about their own history.[54]

For resonant reasons, I believe the women of the Hroswitha Club were motivated to gather and create mechanisms for mutual validation and kinship. Ruth Granniss' experience with the Grolier Club as its long-term librarian underscored her belief that private book clubs were valid forms of scholarly research and contribution to the history of the book. She argues, "Bibliography is indebted to private book clubs for the books about books which they publish, for the exhibitions which they hold, for the libraries which they form, and for the love of books which they foster."[55] While the Hroswitha Club's activities would be markedly different from the Grolier Club's, they certainly incorporated this same amount of scholarly expertise and love of books.

---

[54] See "Coeducation: History of Women at Princeton University." Holden's views are expressed throughout her letters, but see specifically Holden, *Address to Hroswitha Club* and Horner, "Record Memorandum to Miriam Young Holden," p. 2.

[55] Granniss, "What Bibliography Owes," p. 33.

3 "And We're Off": Meetings and Activities

The Hroswitha Club's activities took place in locations ranging from Boston to Baltimore with a special emphasis on New York City and Philadelphia. During its tenure, the club met more than 200 times, and a typical meeting would consist of a short business session where the group would discuss membership or the funding of various projects, a luncheon, and a lecture and display of a member or guest's books.

As a sample, on November 14, 1946, they met in New Haven, Connecticut, and were hosted by Anne "Annie" Lewis, who with her husband Wilmarth "Lefty" Lewis founded the Lewis Walpole Library at Yale University. Anne was like many of the early Hroswithians: financially stable and a serious collector. They had "three separate libraries with 25,000 18th cen[tury] books, pamphlets, manuscripts & bound volumes relating to [Horace] Walpole," according to *The New Yorker*.[56] Anne was the daughter of an oil executive who seemed to happily suffer from bibliophilia. In that, the Lewises were a pair: Anne "was completely identified with [Wilmarth] in all his work," devoting her own time and fortune to the libraries.[57] When she died in 1959, Wilmarth wrote, "That she was balanced and generous was immediately obvious to all who met her, but her modesty concealed great knowledge and insight."[58] Anne's papers are in the Lewis Walpole and gesture to her involvement in local heritage and historical societies and social welfare groups such as the Red Cross.[59]

On this visit, the Lewises hosted a luncheon before a presentation of Yale Library's holdings by Gilbert Troxell, curator of American literature and a bibliographer, who gave them a tour of the library and displayed some of its manuscripts. His wife, Janet Troxell, was a Hroswithian and expert on the Rossettis.[60] After the tour and lecture, the group retired to the Elizabethan Club, a salon on Yale's campus known colloquially at *the Lizzy* that houses a library of Early Modern English literature. Gilbert Troxell was the club's librarian and published on its unique focus on

---

[56] See Hellman. [57] See Hellman and *The New York Times* "Wilmarth S. Lewis."
[58] Quoted in Walker, "Doing Good by Stealth." [59] See Markham.
[60] See Fraser.

allowing undergraduate students to work with rare books.[61] The Lizzy was usually reserved to its male undergraduate members and associated faculty, but the influence of Gilbert and the Lewises opened the club's doors and the Hroswithians were able to examine the Lizzy's holdings along with their tea.[62] Bartlett, who had worked extensively with the library, gave an impromptu lecture. In her description of the events, Anne Haight characterizes Bartlett as "the great authority on the bibliographical points of the editions of Shakespeare" while emphasizing the erudition of the presentation.[63]

Many meetings would follow this pattern of a mixture of frivolity, tea, and sharing of expertise. The Club was able to access materials for study they might not otherwise be allowed to handle by leaning on relationships, as with the Lewises and Troxells. Similarly, in January 1948, Greene hosted the group at the Morgan Library and "kindly said that we had full freedom to enter the vaults and examine treasures at will."[64] Acting secretary Emily Gildersleeve English writes, "It would be impossible to describe the interest which the members derived from the rare privilege of taking in their hands and looking over the many books and manuscripts, some of inestimable value, or to enumerate the wealth of rarities thus opened to the members."[65] These included illuminated books of hours and other incunables. While Greene's kindness is emphasized in the meeting minutes, she had spent years building the Morgan's collection – her trust in the group was likely reflective of their own experience with rare book handling and care.

The "rarities" that the Hroswithians handled were collected thanks to Greene's skill and keen eye for manuscripts, which had grown the Morgan into its impressive state as a research library. In 1930, Bartlett wrote to Greene that despite the fact the library was more well-known for incunables, "The Morgan Library with its magnificent Caxtons and other early English Shakespeares and fine plays and many other outstanding books is

---

[61] See Troxell. [62] My thanks to Basie Gitlin for his insight into the club's history.

[63] Haight, "Minutes of the Hroswitha Club," November 1946, n.p.

[64] English "Minutes of the Hroswitha Club," January 1948, n.p.

[65] English "Minutes of the Hroswitha Club," January 1948, n.p.

the best collection we have in New York."[66] Greene's papers show her shrewd managing of other dealers, collectors, and auctions, as evidenced by this exchange with Ernst Philip Goldschmidt, an antiquarian book dealer who Greene worked with often:

> In regard to Lot 14 in the Phillipps sale, Nov. 11 [1946], [Abraham S. W.] Rosenbach has just telephoned me that, unless we want to get it, he will buy it. He had the same word of price – £150 – from Sotheby and says that is just a stall. He says that he saw the leaf at the Phillipps place and offered £2000. for it – and was laughed to scorn.
>
> My idea is that Sotheby put the £150 on – knowing that it that it [sic] would not be allowed to leave England.
>
> I am bidding £250. through Rosenbach to appease – or anger him. He is disgusted (left no doubt of that!) and I do not doubt that before the sale, he will telephone me that he will not accept that bid.[67]

Greene's observations are both clever and erudite with a characteristic rhetorical underlining. She is referring to a Sotheby's sale of Sir Thomas Phillipps' library that featured as Lot 14 the original vellum manuscript of the Charter of Wihtred, King of Kent, from 699.[68] The manuscript was purchased for £160, less than the tongue-in-cheek £250 Greene offered or the £2000 from Rosenbach, by Sir Albert Stern and donated to the Kent History and Library Centre. Rosenbach (who was known as "The Terror of the Auction Room" at Sotheby's[69]) believes the auction house is stalling,

---

[66] Bartlett, "Letter to Belle Da Costa Greene," January 1930, n.p. In her reply, Greene identifies Bartlett as "the authority" on English literature, which will help her convince the board to purchase more early English books.

[67] Greene, "Letter to Ernst Philip Goldschmidt, October 1946, n.p.

[68] See *Bibliotheca Phillippica*. My thanks to the Grolier Club for providing access to this document, which as the selling price annotated on it. Sotheby's was not able to confirm due to privacy guidelines.

[69] "Abraham Simon Wolf Rosenbach," p. 115.

but Greene correctly suspects that the manuscript was underpriced because it never intended to leave the country. The charter is an important piece of English history,[70] and it clearly would have sold for more than £160 if deep-pocketed American collectors and libraries had a run at it. As the sale was in November 1946 and there is a 1947 article on the manuscript at Kent, Stern likely bought and immediately donated it to the library on the land where the charter was written and signed.

In February 1950, there is a similar display of collecting expertise melding with political machinations; after all, book collecting was "the hunt." This meeting was hosted by Alice Brayton with a lecture and exhibit of Harriet Chapman Sprague's collection of Walt Whitman. Brayton is one of the more eccentric of the club's members, judging from what can be gleaned from meeting minutes. She lived in Portsmouth, Rhode Island, at Brayton House on Green Animals Topiary Garden, known for its extensive shaped topiaries. A giraffe topiary once held court at the table during meeting when the Hroswitha Club traveled to Rhode Island with an odd number. Brayton never married and contributed to historical societies and wrote books about local history, such as *George Berkeley in Newport* (1954). Very importantly, Brayton knew how to throw a party. She hosted a fabulous luncheon at the Colony Club, a private women's social club with activist roots. Haight, as secretary, describes the scene as follows:

> Beautiful white lilacs were flown from Holland for the occasion. Champaigne [sic] bottles were placed on the table as a symbol of frivolity and little dolls represented the members, each holding a miniature book in which their names were inscribed. A bust of Abraham Lincoln stood appropriately in front of Mrs. Frank Sprague, and the chef had made a magnificent cake marked "Hroswitha" and surrounded by pink roses. A record of "Brush up your Shakespeare" from the musical comedy "Kiss Me Kate" was played as a suggestion for a theme song, and

[70] See Ward.

> Miss Brayton had prepared a clever questionnaire on Walt
> Whitman, to which, Mrs. Sprague of course knew all the
> answers.[71]

The conspicuous consumption of the lunch with personalized dolls, inter-
nationally delivered lilacs, and bottles of champagne blends with an ever-
present erudition. The song in the background emphasizes the playfulness
of the event, and one can imagine champagne mixing with lyrics like "Brush
up your Shakespeare / And the women you will wow" and about a dozen
innuendos that suggest a feminine erotics attached to literary knowledge.
The quiz about Whitman preempted Sprague's lecture and display of her
exceptional collection, which was exhibited at the Library of Congress in
1939 and the University of Pennsylvania in 1942.[72] The minutes detail
Sprague's growing interest in Whitman: "During a literary discussion at
tea [with a friend in Cambridge], Mrs. Sprague was asked how she liked
Whitman . . . her interest was aroused and she determined to learn more of
this great American poet whom the English admired so much."[73] Her
collection began with an unopened copy of *Leaves of Grass* and soon grew
to one of two preeminent Whitman collections in the country.

While the meeting minutes indicate the collection will be left to the
Library of Congress, it was in fact already sold to Penn in 1944 – likely on
loan to Sprague for this event.[74] Lynne Farrington, Senior Curator of
Special Collections at Penn, hypothesizes that the shift to Penn from the
Library of Congress was due to several factors, the most significant of
which is that Penn professor Edward Sculley Bradley was working on an
edition of Whitman's *Leaves of Grass*. Bradley praises Sprague's collection
as essential: "This edition will require reference to the many editions of
Leaves of Grass, and there is nowhere else in any one collection such an
unbroken sequence of these as Mrs. Sprague has assembled. No doubt her

---

[71] Haight, "Minutes of the Hroswitha Club," February 1950, n.p.

[72] Sprague, *A List of Manuscripts, Books, Portraits, Prints, Broadsides and
Memorabilia*.

[73] Haight, "Minutes of the Hroswitha Club," February 1950, n.p.

[74] For more on the collection, see Smith.

collection will ultimately simplify one of the most difficult and urgent tasks to be performed by American scholarship."[75] An additional factor is that Sprague may have wanted to differentiate her work from the Thomas Biggs Harned collection already at the Library of Congress.[76] Sprague's "greatest coup" was purchasing Anne Gilchrest's family's side of the correspondence with Whitman,[77] and keeping these documents separate from Harned's would allow her accomplishment to remain distinct.

While lunches were frequently less splashy than Brayton's fête, the scholarly portions of the club's activities were as often focused on truly one-of-a-kind lectures and visits. These women's collections, expertise, and access to institutional resources are impressive for women of this period, or really any period. A list of all their meeting places would include most of the major libraries and many of the notable private collections on the East Coast, including Yale, Harvard, Princeton, the University of Virginia, Bryn Mawr, the Walter's Art Gallery in Washington, DC, Carnegie Mellon, Philadelphia Museum of Art, Two River Farm in Branchburg, New Jersey, and the library of Thomas W. Streeter, as a sample. Exhibits were usually done for their benefit, with the collectors arranging books that represented their libraries or on a topic they thought would be interesting to the club – often on women writers or women's history, such as when they visited the Library of Congress in April 1955. These events were all consuming, according to Frances Milliken Hooper, who joined the club in 1965 and is known equally for her collections and being an early woman advertising executive. Hooper wrote, "You and the collections of the day and collector-members are on intimate terms in a way that aren't really intimate but akin to it, for you temporarily forget all else in the glow of all being interested at the same time in the collection being shown and talked about."[78] One can imagine the collective energy in the room as they danced to "Brush Up Your Shakespeare" or gathered in hushed but excited tones in the Morgan's vault.

When they visited Princeton in 1968, their second visit, it was similarly designed to be memorable, both for the Hroswithians and the library. They

---

[75] See Bradley, p. 37. [76] Farrington, Lynn 2022. pers. comm.
[77] Farrington, "Collecting Whitman," n.p. [78] Hooper, *Collector in Being*, n.p.

were hosted by Charles Ryskamp, a professor of English and friend of Anne Haight and other Hroswithians as he worked for both the Morgan and the Frick. The meeting minutes, written by an unknown hand, describe the meeting:

> Dr. Ryskamp had very carefully thought out the program and called it "Hroswitha Day" ... [Dr. William Dix and Dr. Edward Rice] made us feel much at home for they had selected examples of books and manuscripts reflecting the special interests of members of the club. These were displayed on tables where they could be handled and examined. ... The small exhibition devoted to Hroswitha and the Hroswitha Club was placed in the main Library so that one saw it at once on entering the building.[79]

Ryskamp hosted a luncheon with the library staff and university administrators that included a printed keepsake, a portion of which is preserved in the winter 1969 edition of the *Princeton Library Chronicle*. Ryskamp's pamphlet fetes the event as "one of the greatest pleasures of the autumn for the Library staff" and details the library's holdings.[80]

This event is noticeable for several reasons, one of which is that the subtext of these meetings becomes more evident: Princeton was courting potential donors like Holden and Troxell. In addition, this was also an auspicious year for Princeton when it formally accepted women in degree-granting programs, and it is likely that the library might be keen on welcoming this new era with some pomp and circumstance. The Hroswitha Club was a well-established women's group with personal ties to the institution, as one of the club's charter members, Eleanor Marquand, was granted an honorary degree from

---

[79] Unknown, "Minutes of the Hroswitha Club," October 1968, n.p. This year's minutes are variously recorded by Anne Haight and Phyllis Gordan. Gordan did not attend this meeting, so the description is likely from Anne Haight, but I cannot be sure as it is unsigned.

[80] Ryskamp, p. 123.

Princeton in 1948.[81] The last important note is Ryskamp's relationship with the Hroswithians, which is reportedly warm and cordial. He is referred to in kind terms for years in meeting minutes. Many members had close ties to the Morgan, so a mutually beneficial relationship is not surprising, but this event indicates how much relationships and courting potential donors shaped the Hroswithians' experiences with institutions like the Lizzy, the Morgan, and Princeton.

As these descriptions indicate, these visits were occasionally marked with a commemorative text, such as Ryskamp's article, *A Brief Account of the Origins and Purpose of the Chapin Library at Williams College. Published in Honor of the Hroswitha Club, May 10th, 1956*, and *Americana-Beginnings: A Selection from the Library of Thomas W. Streeter Shown in Honor of a Visit for the Hroswitha Club on May 3, 1951*. Another such pamphlet was produced in 1960 when Miriam Holden addressed her fellow Hroswithians when they visited her personal library in New York. Born in Boston in 1893, Holden was an activist, largely tied to women's issues and organizations like Planned Parenthood, but she was also active in the Urban League and Junior League. She attended Simmons College and took courses on social work but did not leave with a degree. Holden's library was comprised of more than 6,000 volumes on the history of women. While she was committed to women's issues in the United States, her interests were wide ranging and extended to Greece, China, and the Byzantine Empire. Similarly to several of the other club members, Holden's library was motivated by a feminist interest in legitimizing women's history through the collecting of women's history.[82] While many collectors focus on aesthetics and ideal copies, Holden was more concerned with use. She prefaced the group: "Please remember when you see my books that I do not have them because they are rare or

---

[81] For more on Marquand and women at Princeton, especially faculty wives, see Armstrong.

[82] For another well-known example of collecting women's history, see Baskin.

because of their value. I collect them only because I hope they contain within them some significant records of women that will be meaningful to those who are seeking and using them."[83]

The talk touched at least one member – Rachel Hunt, who was the club's second president.[84] Born in Pennsylvania in 1882, Hunt was a collector of herbals and an accomplished bookbinder influenced by the arts and crafts movement. She founded Lehcar Bindery in her home, and her bindings feature a monogram of a lamb with the initials "RMcMM."[85] Hunt wrote Holden shortly after the Hroswitha Club visit, saying

> Thank you so much for a delightful afternoon. Not only that, but your very scholarly and erudite paper on WOMEN touched my heart. I really meant what I said that I thought your article should be published as, perhaps, a "keepsake". You were wonderful to do this for the Hroswitha Club. I think it is one of our high spots, and no one appreciated your work more than I did.[86]

The keepsake was the pamphlet, which Hunt had printed and distributed. Holden and Hunt were avocational collectors, and they recognized the expertise that each has built through a life of engaging with rare book and objects. Hunt characterizes Holden's talk as "scholarly," and Holden thanks her with "I have always felt that you were especially discerning, so that I was <u>more</u> than pleased to have won your approval."[87] As this example illustrates, for many of the members the Hroswitha Club functioned as a network of validation and connection in the absence of institutional

---

[83] Holden, "Address to the Hroswitha Club." For more on Holden's library, see Lerner and Ozment.

[84] "Rachel McMasters Miller Hunt."

[85] "Rachel McMasters Miller Hunt: Plantswoman, Bookwoman, Craftswoman."

[86] Hunt, "Thank You Card," February 1960.

[87] Young, "Letter to Mrs. [Rachel] Hunt," February 1960, n.p. Emphasis in original.

affiliations that recognized men and men's work. Holden and Hunt both had the motivation and means to change this dynamic through their collections and financial support, and their large-scale changes matched the small ways they supported each other and the women collectors and activists in their lives.

4 "The Abiding Love of Books": Relationships and Networks

In meeting minutes, there is a constant interplay between sharing scholarly information and partaking in the joy of fellowship and shared interests. A lecture will be bookended by a generously hosted luncheon, congratulations about a recent endeavor, reports of new grandchildren, well-wishes for a sick member, and, more frequently as the years went on, obituaries. The minutes illuminate that the club was a space for women to teach, to learn, and to share in intimacy with books as collectable objects and as possibilities for self-enrichment. It is these relationships that are perhaps the most important but ephemeral part of their story. Book collecting usually happens through networks of dealers, friends, and fellow collectors, and these relationships can be difficult to track. Some collectors like Eccles and curators like Greene keep meticulous records of who they bought from and where, but many more have been lost to recycling bins and email folders. One might imagine that Rachel Hunt's support of Miriam Holden's talk was not atypical; it is simply that Holden saved it and had enough clout to have her papers preserved in a library. This section traces a select few Hroswithians' networks that have been captured through oral histories, obituaries, and memoirs as a signifier of the relationality that was key to this group's life. Taken together, these accounts emphasize the informal apprenticeships that formed spaces for women's training as collectors and bibliophiles.

While New York was the club's home, there was a significant contingent in Rhode Island, especially Providence. Several Rhode Island Hroswithians joined early on: Alice Brayton and Margaret Stillwell in 1944 and Anne S. K. Brown in 1949. They were joined by Beatrice "Happy" Chace in 1963 and Rebecca More in 1971. As one might imagine, geographic vicinity was an important factor for these networks. Providence is home to Brown University, which Anne Brown had family ties to and where More and Stillwell worked. More offered her perspective on how book collecting and value in the knowledge that books could give brought these members together.[88]

---

[88] More, Rebecca 2022. pers. comm.

More remembers her entrance to book collecting as a mixture of personal inclination and deliberate mentorship. She collected books from her teenage years, going on dates with her husband Timothy, who was interested in architecture, at secondhand bookshops. Her collection consists of cookbooks and books on botany, which she still holds in their historic home in Providence. An interest in bibliophilia was nurtured early on by Wilmarth "Lefty" Lewis. Lefty was close friends with More's grandfather and prompted her to think seriously about her collections. When More would visit the Lewis' house in Farmington, Connecticut, she would "have the run of the library" and learned about bibliography and old books from handling the Lewis' materials. This informal but essential learning has echoes of Henrietta Bartlett's education in Beverly Chew's library and Jane Quinby in Rachel Hunt's library.

The Mores moved to Charlottesville, Virginia, in the 1960s where Rebecca met Mary Preston Massey in the jam aisle at the grocery store. Mary and her husband Linton were both collectors; Linton Massey was a member of the Grolier Club, and Mary Massey was one of the first women admitted in the 1970s. Linton Massey knew William Faulkner and amassed a collection of Faulkner's works and their correspondence which were deposited at the University of Virginia.[89] Mary Massey collected herbals and donated 330 of her books to the Folger Shakespeare Library in 1994.[90] The collection includes books from the fifteenth through the twentieth centuries and examples from Europe and North America in multiple languages. Their daughter Frances Converse Massey was also admitted to both the Grolier Club and Hroswitha Club as a collector of books, iconography of pigs, and the work of Edward Gorey. Mary Massey took on a mentorship role to More, and the families met socially while the Mores lived in Charlottesville. Adding to the foundation Lefty Lewis had helped establish, Mary Massey encouraged More in her collecting and to consider it as more than a hobby. It was Mary Massey who nominated More for

---

[89] Special Collections Department Staff, "Guide to Linton R. Massey Papers."

[90] The Folger's catalog Hamnet lists Massey as a former owner of 330 herbals. An exhibit catalog of her collection was printed in 1988. See *The Grete Herball: Books from the Collection of Mary P. Massey*.

membership to Hroswitha Club in 1971, a membership More held until the club dissolved in 2004. A thirty-year membership was achieved by more than one Hroswithian, including Anne Brown, Sarah Larkin Loening, Emily English, and Jane Wild Howe, who was a member for an impressive fifty-three years. More was admitted when she was younger than most members and many of her mentors were older women collectors who took her under their wings and allowed her to imagine collecting as a path for self-actualization and an important mechanism for learning more about one's chosen topic.

Anne Brown was one such mentor, who the Mores met formally when they moved to Providence in 1970. While they moved for Timothy's career as a lawyer, Providence was attractive partially because of its historical architecture. They are the second owners of their eighteenth-century house, the oldest on Benefit Street in College Hill in its original location, where they have lived since 1970.[91] Being a member of the Hroswitha Club helped connect the Mores to other bibliophiles in Providence, and it led to a "tremendous opportunity" of working in Brown's collection of more than 100,000 books, prints, and other items, most of which is now in the John Hay and John Carter Brown libraries. More remembers Mrs. Brown as a formidable figure at around 6 feet tall in full fur coats who employed librarians and catalogers to work in her extensive private library. Brown hired More, who had a bachelor's degree in history from the University of Virginia, as a subject indexer. As More worked through the Austrian, Belgian, and Swedish collections, she developed her training as a collector and historian, learning to handle primary sources and material books with care and bibliographic precision. Partially because of this experience, More went on to earn additional degrees, and she noticed a difference in how her background shaped her engagement in historical research. "My approach to historical source material was much more catholic than most of my contemporaries," she recalls. "I realized prints and drawings can be just as useful a window into historical analysis [as books]." In the libraries of Lefty

[91] Benefit Street is a notable historical center in Providence, and tourists can go on walking tours of the homes. Stillwell gave a talk on the area for Hroswitha Club in 1965 and published *The Pageant of Benefit Street* in 1943 and 1945.

Lewis and Anne Brown and through the mentorship of Mary Massey, More learned about bibliography and historical research with hands-on apprenticeships that would shape her career as a historian of sixteenth- and seventeenth-century English self-governance and social values.

Another Hroswithian in More's mentor network was Beatrice "Happy" Chace, who joined the Hroswitha Club in 1963 and was a member until her death in 1992. Chace graduated from Smith College in 1928 and collected American authors like Willa Cather and Ernest Hemingway. She had several children, including daughters who endowed a garden and a library fund in their mother's name. Chace was a book collector, but her primary passion was preservation of historical architecture in Providence. Chace cofounded the Providence Preservation Society, for which she has been inducted into the Rhode Island Heritage Hall of Fame and was honored by the Rhode Island School of Design Museum with the Chace Center. Chace decided to personally invest in the College Hill neighborhood by buying and renovating forty homes in a block that the *New York Times* reports "came to be called Happy Land."[92] This movement was part of a "Renaissance" in Providence, which has continued into the present.[93] As a fellow inhabitant of College Hill, More met Chace when she moved into her Benefit Street home and Chace was inspiring to the burgeoning historian for her commitment to preserving architecturally significant homes. More recalls that Chace did not do this work for the money, which she did not need, but because she wanted to see her neighborhood thrive and wanted to contribute to the community that she called home.

While family ties and chance encounters are a part of this story, it was importantly through the Hroswitha Club that More and these women

[92] Klemesrud, p. 8. The displacement of poor families is noted in the *New York Times* piece, and the Providence Preservation Society has since addressed this issue on its website: "Our reputation has been built on revitalizing historic neighborhoods in Providence, which has had profound consequences for many people who lacked resources and power, many of whom were people of color." See "Providence Preservation Society" for more.

[93] See Leazes and Garrahy.

shared a sense of connection and fellowship. "They were a lively, wonderful group of people" More said. "These were women for whom there were no expectations who created for themselves intellectual lives and tried to make contributions to the intellectual and cultural lives of their communities, whether local or more national or international." Hroswithians' relationship to book collecting varied from women who just loved books to serious collectors, but throughout there is a strand of women creating a space for their self-actualization by solving community-level problems and building relational networks in their neighborhoods and abroad.

A resonantly similar story plays out between Julia Wightman and Chantal Hodges, which is captured in interviews taken by Elizabeth Denlinger. These women were part of the large New York contingent of the club, and Wightman was one of the most consistent and prominent members. She was admitted in 1955 and was a member until her death in 1994. She was a recording secretary and later president from 1978 to 1994, and it is her materials that I primarily worked through at the Grolier Club. She was admitted to the Grolier Club in 1977, and as a fellow of the Morgan Library she had close ties to that institution as well. The Morgan has Wightman's collection of miniature books and bindings and some of her other bequests and papers, as she highly valued the institution: "she gave the best things to the Morgan; when a book or binding was at a certain level of rarity or extraordinary quality, she saw it, even in her lifetime, as properly belonging at the Morgan."[94] As often happens with close benefactors and institutions, Wightman and the Morgan forged a "kind of intimacy, arising from affection for both the objects and the institution."[95] Wightman would frequently pledge money for collections and books at the request of Morgan curators. As with Miriam Holden, Rachel Hunt, Happy Chace, and many other Hroswithians, Denlinger argues that Wightman "was keenly aware that she was collecting for future generations. Her two occupations of

---

[94] Denlinger, "Julia Parker Wightman," p. 7–8.
[95] Denlinger, "Julia Parker Wightman," p. 8.

binder and collector came together in the many book boxes she made: the practice allowed her to work on beautiful things of tooled and gilt leather without permanently imprisoning books or damaging them."[96]

Wightman's ideas about collecting for the future extended to her work with the Hroswitha Club. She was close with several Hroswithians, including Deborah Evetts, a Morgan bookbinder who joined in 1980, and Chantal Hodges, who joined in 1977. Wightman sponsored both for membership.

Wightman mentored Hodges in the same ways that Brown and Massey took on an unofficial apprenticeship of More. Wightman told Hodges "she had an eye for books," brought her into the Hroswitha Club, and took her book shopping around New York.[97] Hodges had a more modest budget than Wightman (most people did), but she collected children's books, including Arthur Rackham, William Heath and Charles Robinson, and Ernest Shepard.[98] This collection grew to more than 1,500 books and earned her admittance to the Grolier Club. Her interest in children's books was born from a nostalgia; Denlinger writes that "This collection preserves not just children's books but the memory of child readers."[99] Hodges died in February 2021, and it is unknown what her family has decided to do with her collection.

While most of these relational networks are either lost or have yet to be uncovered in papers and family collections, the club's formal meeting minutes also went out of their way to codify memories of fellow collectors for both posterity and to preserve in writing the kinship that these women formed. "In Memoriam" obituaries are inserted and distributed with the minutes, interleaving happy accounts of outings with solemn but joyful remembrances. The Hroswitha

---

[96] Denlinger, "Julia Parker Wightman," p. 9.
[97] Denlinger, "Some Women Book Collectors," p. 3.
[98] Denlinger, "Some Women Book Collectors," p. 3.
[99] Denlinger, "Some Women Book Collectors," p. 4.

Club's library, which will be discussed in the next section, was named in memorial for their first president Sarah Gildersleeve Fife, who died in 1949. When Belle Greene died in 1950, the club remembered her in an obituary and with frequent mentions to her in the meeting minutes. An unsigned memorial blends an affection for Greene's generosity with her intellect:

> No one who knew her would ever forget her vivid and many-sided personality, her kindness and thoughtfulless [sic], her sense of fun and her whole-hearted devotion to the great institution [Morgan Library] of which she was almost the founder ... Her insight and flair made her one of the great collectors ... while her basic humility of mind helped her to use the best of brains of her time and won their complete collaboration.[100]

A similar pattern follows for Rachel Hunt, who died in 1963 shortly after the club traveled to Pittsburgh to see her library at Carnegie Mellon endowed. Her club obituary was written by her friend Margaret Stillwell: "We knew her as a collector of rare books, as a skilled book-binder, as an active participant in civic betterment. ... In the Hroswitha Club she found not only affection but that special kinship that collectors have with one another who, in spite of varied interests, share together the abiding love of books."[101]

For a few Hroswithians, these memorials give more information than official obituaries or legacy pages. Such is the case of Elizabeth Frelinghuysen, who died in 1983. She was born in Boston and was active in the New Jersey Historical Society and the Society of Preservation of New England Antiquities among other groups, and she was committed to

---

[100] Haight, "Minutes of the Hroswitha Club," May 2, 1950, n.p. The quote after the first ellipsis is attributed to William George Constable of the Boston Museum of Fine Arts.

[101] Quoted in Wightman, "Minutes of Hroswitha Club," November 1963, n.p.

historical restoration.[102] In particular, she focused on Gunston Hall, the eighteenth-century estate of George Mason. Elizabeth M. Riley wrote Frelinghuysen's obituary and similarly highlighted both her admiration for Frelinghuysen's scholarly work and fellowship in the club.

> She was indefatigable in her researches, combing lists, examining collections, dealing with dealers in England as well as New Jersey, to find the books that would have been in the library of the time of George Mason of Gunston Hall. Charles Ryskamp ... says her diligence in tracking down books for this collection was extraordinary, and set high standards for similar restorations.[103]

While Frelinghuysen was publicly active enough in named institutions, and from a prominent enough family, to earn a *New York Times* obituary, her obituary from the Hroswitha Club is much more familiar and emphasizes not just the societies she joined, but the work she did and the care with which she did it.

Similarly, the memorial for Eleanor Towne Carey captures what public textual traces do not. Carey was born in 1901 in New York and collected medieval literature and sculptures. She joined the club in 1971 but was only briefly a member, as she died suddenly in 1972 while traveling in Norway. According to her obituary, written by Hannah Howell, who was the art librarian at the Frick,[104] Carey undertook a good deal of bibliographic work when she acquired a copy of Jacobus de Voragine's *Legenda Aurea* printed in Venice in 1492 by Matteo Capcasa. The incunable was one of only a few known copies, and Carey traveled to Italy to verify which she now owned: "Mrs. Carey saw and studied each of the known copies, consulted with the librarians in each city and collected the records to verify the incunabulum as the lost copy from the [Francesco] Melzi Library.

---

[102] "Elizabeth Frelinghuysen Dies," p. 10.   [103] Riley, "In Memoriam," n.p.
[104] See "Hannah J. Howell."

She presented the book, just a few months before her death to the Morgan Library."[105]

Carey's donation was not marked in the Morgan's catalog but in verifying it for this study, curator John McQuillen added the accession information.[106] Carey has next to no textual traces of the rest of her collections as they were reportedly left to her two children after her sudden death, and she was much less well-known than her husband. This is not an atypical story for Hroswithians whose collections did not attract newspaper articles with splashy donations that research libraries depend on to attract more donations. As with the de Voragine at the Morgan, they could be in libraries without donation tags visible to the public.

In addition to the warmth and care that is interwoven throughout the obituaries, for Carey, Frelinghuysen, and many other women these memorials are some of the only records of their lives as collectors. So few are included in references like Donald Dickson's *Dictionary of American Book Collectors* and Joseph Rosenblum's *American Book-Collectors and Bibliographers*, and they were unable to access institutions like universities that would have yearbooks and other traces. Hroswithians wrote a history of each other's lives and scholarly labor so that someone, somewhere would know that Alice Brayton was a "Fairy Godmother" to Marjorie Barlow's daughter, that "She had a remarkable personality, gay with great knowledge and an all-embracing enjoyment of people, places and books."[107] The Hroswithians bear witness that Katharine Starr Oliver's "interests were so varied and her knowledge so encompassing, she might be called a 'polyperson.'"[108] Along these personally written obituaries and memorials are newspaper clippings of members' activities and notices, kept by club members to honor their friends. Throughout the minutes, passed but remembered names appear frequently. When the club published

---

[105] Howell, "In Memoriam," n.p.

[106] My thanks to Sal Robinson, Assistant Curator of Historical Manuscripts at the Morgan Library & Museum for her help with this query.

[107] Barlow, "In Memoriam" n.p. [108] Young, "In Memoriam," n.p.

Hroswitha of Gandersheim in 1965, it was through Roy Hunt's support in the name of his late wife, and the volume was dedicated to Rachel.

Given the formality of the meeting minutes and the ever-present propriety and carefulness in their language, it is unlikely if any tension or spats would be recorded, so I do not position this history as unbiased or comprehensive. It does, however, emphasize the importance of interpersonal ties of book collecting that dovetailed with the relationality of a women's social club to create a culture where women's bibliophilic excellence was fostered.

5 "Of Maximum Usefulness": Publications and Projects

Fitting the tenor of a club focused on personal enrichment, fellowship, and erudition, for several projects the group gathered their resources to collaborate on more public-facing projects: a library and three publications. The library was one of the club's earliest projects, the brainchild of Sarah Fife, the first president, in December 1948:

> The Secretary [Anne Haight] told of Mrs. Fife's great desire to form a Hroswitha Club library composed of books written by members and books which would be of permanent interest. Mrs. [Rachel] Hunt announced that if the Club so desired she would present a first edition of the plays of Hroswitha as the cornerstone of a collection to be known as "The Sarah Fife Library."[109]

Fife was ill and did not attend this meeting, nor any future ones; she died in May 1949, and the library became her memorial. Most of the library remains intact at the Grolier Club, although it moved around from members' homes to the Colony Club and the Morgan Library over the years. The Morgan also kept the club's archive until it was moved to the Grolier Club. The initial donation was thirty books in January 1949, and the books ranged from creative works authored by Sarah Larkin to extensive tomes of bibliographic labor from Haight, Bartlett, Troxell, and Bertha Coolidge Slade. There were also personally written and published books on family and local history.[110] This rather impressive list of books emphasizes again that the "amateur" identity of the members was always a bit of a suspect distinction; while most of these women did not have institutional privileges or formal education, they had through their collecting amassed a significant amount of knowledge on their chosen topics and were producing surveys of bibliographic works that are still used and have since been absorbed into

---

[109] Haight, "Minutes of the Hroswitha Club," December 1948, n.p.
[110] Haight, "Minutes of the Hroswitha Club," January 1949, n.p. Bartlett's papers also include library lists.

WorldCat and other institutional structures. Over the years, members would continue to deposit the fruits of their labor into the library and make gifts in honor of one another; for example, when Greene died, she bequeathed several volumes to Haight for the library. Members served as librarians, specifically Jane Quinby and Marjorie Barlow. The Grolier Club's finding aid has notes for which books were a part of the original Sarah Gildersleeve Fife Memorial Library.[111]

Alongside the library, the group participated in the production of three publications: a biography of Hrosvitha in 1947, a contextual biography, a bibliographical checklist for Hrosvitha's works in 1965, and *Notes on Women Printers*, which is similar to a historical encyclopedia, in 1976. The first is a forty-page pamphlet written by Robert Herndon Fife; all copies I have examined are bound with a blue wrapper, printed on Georgian ivory laid paper, and stab-sewn. Robert Fife was a scholar of German history and culture, and thus the club asked him to produce the pamphlet on Hrosvitha's life with some brief information about her works for their own information and as a keepsake for the club. As a frontispiece, they used an illustration of a woodcut by Albrecht Dürer depicting Hrosvitha presenting her plays to the Otto I of the Holy Roman Empire. This would later be incorporated into the club's letterhead. The pamphlet was funded by the club but designed and produced through Columbia University Press; this choice was partially driven by their desire to have the pamphlet purchased by academic libraries across the country. They also gifted it to libraries and institutions that hosted their visits.

This pamphlet seems to have inspired another, longer project on Hrosvitha – a 1965 checklist of her work titled *Hroswitha of Gandersheim: Her Life, Times, and Work, and a Comprehensive Bibliography*. This book was ambitious in size and scope, and it took up a dozen members' activities for almost a decade, including world travel to examine manuscripts, commissioning microfilm, and completing translations. It showcased the members' own abilities rather than relying on a useful spouse – although they frequently relied on their well-connected and educated spouses to access the documents they needed and arrange for necessary translations. This project

---

[111] Grolier Club, "Hroswitha Club: Records and Publications, 1944–1999."

was truly a collaboration across the club, and they intended it to be a work of scholarship.

It seems to have begun when Marjorie Dana Barlow compiled a list of the Hrosvitha volumes in the Fife Memorial Library in 1955. The club was enthusiastic about Barlow's short list, and it sparked a larger idea. In early 1956, she agreed to compile a complete bibliography of Hrosvitha's works using the club's library as a starting point. Barlow's simple survey became a collaboratively authored, hard-bound bibliography printed in a 1,200-copy run by Bertram L. Clarke and David Way of Thistle Press. They were bibliographical publishers who designed museum catalogs, and the club was particularly happy to have them handle the book's design.[112] As with many scholarly works, the volume suffered from scope creep and enjoyed the "whoosh" of many missed deadlines – they thought the book would come out in 1961, then 1962, and so on.

For the bibliographic work, Barlow was joined by Meta Harrsen, Keeper Emeritus of Manuscripts at the Morgan Library, and Jane Quinby, the Fife librarian and an accomplished cataloger who was responsible for logging the entirety of Rachel Hunt's botanical library. Haight was the lead editor, and she wrote a contextual history of Hrosvitha. Haight's introduction was mentioned in meeting minutes for years, as she kept working on it because there was more to find and she wanted it to be reflective of contemporary literary and historical scholarship. The others seemed to also find this project all-encompassing, and they dedicated themselves to collation, provenance, and dating Hrosvitha's manuscripts and later printings. They corresponded with libraries in Europe to have unphotographed manuscripts turned into microfilm, a few times paying for the associated costs themselves. As one example of this and their process, in 1960 Quinby and Barlow reported that

> After three months of waiting and writing letters to the University of Budapest Library, a microfilm copy of the Ms. used for the 1874 publication was received on April 23. Black and white photographs will be made of the microfilm

[112] Bull, "Minutes of the Hroswitha Club," November 1964, n.p.

for Miss Harrsen. . . . She will be able to verify whether the
1510–1520 date which we now assign to this Ms. is correct or
not.[113]

As editor, Haight checked and double-checked with bibliographers,
German-language experts, and Hrosvitha experts at the Morgan, Grolier,
Houghton, and Hunt libraries as well as several in Europe as part of a self-
directed peer review. They also relied on Margaret Stillwell's expertise as
a bibliographer of incunables.[114] The November 1961 meeting minutes list
much of the work done by different women, ranging from Harrsen's
bibliographic descriptions of Hrosvitha's manuscripts to Mildred Bliss'
arrangement of a translation of contemporary Russian scholarship to
Barlow tracking down previously unknown play performances.[115] In addition to corresponding with various libraries, Barlow herself traveled to
Europe in 1958, and Quinby reported that their work was achieving an
"enormous amount of respect."[116]

In the preface, Haight writes that the volume was intended to, among
other things, "establish the authenticity of Hrosvitha's manuscripts" given
that doubt was cast on the author's existence.[117] Haight comments that the
"long-enduring controversy could have been solved had anyone made
a paleographical examination of the known manuscripts. It remained for the
Hroswitha Club to do so."[118] Harrsen's bibliographical work, in conversation
with the other club members, showed that there was evidence of Hrosvitha's
authorship prior to when she was supposedly invented.[119] They also designed

---

[113] Quinby and Barlow, "Miss Jane Quinby's Report on Progress to Mrs. Barlow,"
n.p.

[114] Stillwell, *Annmary Brown Memorial* and "Margaret Bingham Stillwell Papers, ca.
1925–1984."

[115] Wightman, "Minutes of the Hroswitha Club," November 1961, n.p. and Haight,
Hroswitha of Gandersheim, preface.

[116] Wightman, "Minutes of the Hroswitha Club," November 1961, n.p.

[117] Haight, *Hroswitha of Gandersheim*, p. x.

[118] Haight, *Hroswitha of Gandersheim*, p. x.

[119] Harrsen, "Report," April 1960, n.p.

the book to be bibliographically specific and descriptive enough that it would be useful for students who could not access the manuscripts themselves, which is repeated throughout the club's notes and reports. This emphasizes that part of the club's intent was to increase scholarly interest in Hrosvitha. That is, by building a library on Hrosvitha' works and writing a thorough bibliography in English, they intended to have more students and collectors in the United States take seriously the contributions of Hrosvitha and, by extension, the Hroswithians as well.

The second major publication was as much of an undertaking. Barlow and Haight were again central figures, this time joined by Miriam Boothby Lawrence and her husband George H. M. Lawrence for collation and formatting, Katharine Oliver as a typist, and Mary Massey who negotiated with the University of Virginia Press for distribution.[120] It was a historical encyclopedia titled *Notes on Women Printers in Colonial America and the United States 1639–1975*, the last year being the year before it was published. It was printed by the press of Abraham Colish in Mount Vernon, New York, who frequently printed volumes for the Grolier Club.[121] It is dedicated to Haight, one of the club's scholars on women printers, and opened with a notice about the club that included information about its origins, library, and the *Hroswitha of Gandersheim* bibliography.

This project was largely driven by Barlow, who was born in 1888 in New York City and was from the Dana family in Vermont. Her father's family was bookish; her uncles established the Elm Tree Press in 1907, and her uncle John Cotton Dana was a prominent public librarian in New Jersey. It is perhaps not surprising she was bookish herself and interested in printing. She collected materials relating to boxing and the works of William Hazlitt in addition to a collection of early women printers in the United States. Similarly to book collecting, printing has been a historically masculinized field that women nevertheless persistently entered and worked in.[122] As such, this

---

[120] Barlow, *Notes on Women Printers*.

[121] Lawson, "The Press of A. Colish Archives."

[122] For more on this topic, see Walkup, "Printing at the Margins." In 2017, Walkup taught a class on women printers for the California Rare Book School which remains unique in its attention to gendered labor in the print industry.

volume seems ideologically resonant with the Hroswitha Club's previous works and Barlow's specific interests. The publication combined historical research with correspondence with printers in all fifty states, which Barlow organized by putting letters in a manila envelope for each state. Barlow sent queries to historical and literary institutions like libraries and universities, asking for names, addresses, and titles of presses. The fifty envelopes of replies – ranging from rather slim responses from Rhode Island to quite a few from New York and California – are in two large, red clamshell boxes in the Hroswitha Club archive and represent a fascinating snapshot of women's printing in the 1970s. Many of the correspondents sent samples of their work along with responses to Barlow's query and geographical information. Librarians sent copies of their scant card catalog entries on women, often lamenting how few there were to send.

Barlow and her collaborators drew their lines narrowly; they defined "printer" to exclude women who merely *worked* for other printers, and they were interested in who specifically printed books.[123] Barlow clarifies that she is looking for "Women are currently or have recently been involved through typesetting or operating a press in the production of a book (the post office defines a book as 24 pages, I believe)."[124] What she got in return is highly representative of the messy work of defining letterpress – most respondents are trying to decide if they "qualify" or not and send a hodgepodge of their projects. In an illustrative example, Lois Rather of Rather Press in Oakland, California, reasoned through whether or not she was a printer when writing to Barlow in 1970:

> What am I? Well, I am really a writer mostly, I guess. I do act as a book designer, printers' devil, proofreader, and active partner in Rather Press, but the only real compositing I have done to date has been decorative–like the enclosed Christmas card! Since some of the women I have named as

---

[123] For the former point, see Lawrence and Lawrence, "Letter to Mrs. [Katharine] Peter Oliver," January 1976, n.p.

[124] Quoted in Rather, "Letter to Marjorie Barlow," August 1974, n.p.

printers do even less than this, I guess you may call me
a printer if you like! Proud to be included![125]

Barlow corresponded with Rather throughout the 1970s about printers in
California, which was (and still is) experiencing a renewed interest in
handpress and offset printing. Rather, whose oral history as a printer and
press papers have been preserved at the University of California,
Berkeley,[126] was a prominent figure of this movement, along with
women like Jane Bissell Grabhorn who worked with her husband's
Grabhorn Press and her own Jumbo Press.[127] Rather's responses show
her intimate knowledge of printing and the slipperiness of gendered
definitions of printing and an arbitrary focus on the "book" as
a definition of what makes a woman printer. Rather responds to
Barlow's definition with, "This would eliminate the hundreds of females
who are employed or 'help out' in professional jobs catering to custo-
mers who want calling cards, stationery, or wedding invitations."[128]
Rather was of course correct – twentieth-century letterpress printers,
just like their historical counterparts, printed much more than books.
Barlow's response is handwritten on the letter: "but occasionally they
printed books."[129] However, Rather's objections are valid; some of the
women who responded to Barlow were certainly letterpress printers but
had not printed a book. One such is Jane G. Tuckerman of Gainesville,
Florida. Tuckerman writes about her excitement about the volume and
her own work with Owl Tree Press, which she founded in 1967 with the
purchase of a 5 × 8 Kelsey press: "I have used it to print many times
since then ... such as stationery decorated with my hand-cut block

---

[125] Rather, "Letter to Marjorie Barlow," December 1970, n.p.

[126] "Finding Aid to the Lois Rather Papers." [127] Grabhorn, "The Colt Press."

[128] Rather, "Letter to Marjorie Barlow," August 1974, n.p.

[129] Rather, "Letter to Marjorie Barlow," August 1974, n.p. Rather signs her name in
blue pen at the bottom, and it seems that the black-ink hand is Barlow's. It is the
same as the other letters in the boxes: she dates the received date at the top. On
this letter, she has several annotations responding to Rather's queries.

prints or cuts made from my drawings, cards, etc. etc. I have not yet printed a book."[130]

While some women demurred from calling themselves a printer as Rather initially did, others claimed it happily as with Tuckerman and Therese Terry of Denver, Colorado, who not only claims the title of *printer* but only hires women as printers:

> We do employ only women printers though we have at various times found it necessary to employ male printers because so few women have attempted to enter this field. We are finding now that more and more women are getting into the printing field, much to our delight ... women are more apt and able at printing than most males. One of the reasons for this is that women are, as a rule, absolute perfectionists! They pay attention to detail which is extremely necessary in order to turn out good quality work. They take a great deal of pride in their work and often times, actually surprise themselves. It seems to me that our gals have not been given the chance to show what they really can do in this particular vein and once given the chance, as we do here, they display an amazing amount of ability.[131]

Several more responses are within this same vein, discussing the rise of indie printing in San Francisco and their pride participating in a trade that was traditionally deemed too masculine. A student worker at the Kentucky University Press, Sheila Maybanks, perhaps best typifies this attitude: "I like myself best with a smock on and printers' ink on my hands – it's a great thing. Barefoot too, I can exert more pressure and more 'swing.'"[132] Maybanks' response takes the image of women barefoot and

---

[130] Tuckerman, "Letter to Marjorie Barlow," May 1976, n.p. Tuckerman was not included in the volume, but it could also be because she wrote too late. Barlow dates the receipt of the letter on June 1, 1976.

[131] Terry, "Letter to Marjorie Barlow," December 1969, n.p.

[132] Maybanks, "Letter to Marjorie Barlow," February 1970, n.p.

in the kitchen and spins it as a barefoot, inky, and gloriously happy woman feeling the strength of her body as it interacts with the press to create a book.

Notes on Women Printers was like any other directory – an impossible task and dated as soon as it was printed. Rather wrote to Barlow in November 1975 that the information she had gathered in September 1974 "is now outdated" as "addresses are indefinite and changing, these present-day Bohemians are hard to locate."[133] The Hroswitha Club struggled to recoup its costs, despite receiving letters of support and admiration from universities like Smith College and organizations like the American Antiquarian Society. Judging from a letter sent from the University of Virginia Press to Mary Massey in 1974, *Hroswitha of Gandersheim* was similarly dubbed a "handsome job" but nevertheless the author "doubts that it could ever have hoped for a very wide sale."[134] Considering how much institutions underwrite scholarly work, it is not surprising that a club without significant institutional support would struggle to fund such projects, and Barlow's book would be the club's last publication. It sits at an important moment in the club's history as it began to transition to a new identity in the 1970s and to think more openly about how it saw its history intersecting with gender and the rare book world beyond their namesake. While they did not have an exhibit hall to host exhibitions in, they did spend what time, money, and expertise they could muster to produce more knowledge about women's engagement with book production, which is its own important legacy.

[133] Rather, "Letter to Marjorie Barlow," November 1975, n.p.
[134] Cowen, "Letter to Mary [Massey]," August 1974, n.p. The letter seems to be signed "Walker" and Cowen writes with his full name elsewhere in the archive. "Mary" is assumed to be Mary Massey, as she was the UVA Press contact for the club, referenced in letters from George Lawrence.

6 "No One Has Time": The Later Years

Struggling publications aligned with some interorganizational changes in the 1970s, which marked a shift in how the Hroswitha Club thought about itself and its mission. Ultimately, this led to the club's disbanding in 2004 with significant decrease in activities in 1994. The club's archives and meeting minutes trace a debate about the group's purpose that is resonant with many women's institutions that were created in response to a male-only institution barring women members. Historically, the Grolier Club and the Hroswitha Club members seem to be on friendly terms; the Grolier Club members frequently invited Hroswithians to exhibits or lectures, especially as so many were Grolier wives and friends, and it temporarily housed the club's library or other documents over the decades before becoming its permanent home in 2004.

Women's participation in the Grolier Club excursions required a very key thing, however: a bookish husband. In her essay "Grolier Watching, By a Lady," Mary Hyde Eccles reflects on her years as the wife of a Grolier Club president, Donald Hyde. "I did not feel deprived; nor do I think the other wives of members did either. We had plenty of privileges, and absolutely no responsibilities," she writes. "I felt badly though about ladies on their own who were ideally qualified to join the club except for their gender ... I did know Belle da Costa Greene and Dorothy Miner, to say nothing of a bright array of contemporaries highly qualified for membership."[135] Eccles is clear-eyed about her status as a guest even while enjoying the bookish learning she gets to partake in. Her examples of adeptly qualified women, Greene and Miner, were Hroswithians, and could be joined by Granniss and Bartlett. Miner joined in 1954 and was active until her death in 1973. She was the keeper of manuscripts at the Walters Art Gallery in Washington, DC and shared with Meta Harrsen, Greene, Stillwell, and a few other members an intimate knowledge of incunables and medieval manuscripts. In addition to their subject-matter knowledge, all these women retained the "Miss" throughout their lives and

---

[135] Eccles, "Grolier Watching, By a Lady," p. 255–256.

did not marry – preventing them, no matter their expertise, from participating in the Grolier Club for more than lady's days and teas.

It was this inequality that attracted the attention of Elizabeth Swaim in 1974.[136] Swaim wrote to then-club president Anne Haight about formally petitioning the Grolier Club to allow women. The meeting minutes detail an unsaved letter:

> The President [Anne Haight] read a communication from Mrs. Elizabeth A. Swain [sic], Middletown, Conn., requesting a statement on the position of the Hroswitha Club relative to The Grolier Club's policy of denying membership to women and the restriction of women to attendance at some functions by invitation only. Ms. Swain's contention was that in function, if not in title, The Grolier Club is no longer strictly a men's social club, but is a professional organization whose interests and activities are germane to women as to men. She expressed the hope that the Hroswitha Club would endorse this viewpoint and give support to her efforts to persuade The Grolier Club Board to expunge all its restrictions against women.[137]

Haight wrote a rely, also unsaved, which "advised Ms. Swain that she was not the slightest bit interested in joining The Grolier Club, that we [the Hroswitha Club] are an ancient and honorable organization with our own ties and have no desire to interfere with The Grolier Club."[138] By 1974, Hroswitha had a thirty-year history, and members' prickliness that there was something lacking in their organization could be understandable, especially from Haight who had been present for thirty years. While they may have started as the "female Grolier" in theory, in practice they rarely

---

[136] I could not find information on an Elizabeth A. Swain, but Elizabeth Denlinger located an Elizabeth Ann Swaim who seems a likely candidate for this writer. See *The Hartford Courant* "Swaim, Elizabeth Ann."

[137] Lawrence, "Minutes of the Hroswitha Club," January 1974, n.p.

[138] Lawrence, "Minutes of the Hroswitha Club," January 1974, n.p.

refered to themselves that way. They had their own identity, rules, norms, and projects.

Swaim was also not incorrect that the Grolier Club's membership and scope had changed and that career women were disadvantaged by not being able to join or attend its lectures, as Eccles glosses in her reflection. Phyllis Goodhart Gordan observed as much and argued that "it was a disadvantage to professionals like herself . . . not to be allowed to belong to the club and participate in activities that were most pertinent to them professionally."[139] Gordan's experience is particularly striking. In 1952, Curt F. Bühler of the Morgan Library and Karl Küp of the New York Public Library curated an exhibit on "Books of the First Half Century of Printing, 1450–1500" that featured selections from the library of Howard Lehman Goodhart, Gordan's father, who was a member of the Grolier Club and died in 1951. Goodhart split his collection of incunables between Bryn Mawr and his daughter, who specialized in the Italian Renaissance and published a bibliographic checklist of his collection that, of course, uses references from Stillwell's foundational work.[140] Gordan loaned some of her father's collections to Bühler and Küp's exhibit, but "was not allowed to be present at the meeting when those bindings were the subject of a featured speaker's address at the opening of the exhibit."[141] Bühler spoke, and the address was later published as *Fifteenth Century Books and the Twentieth Century*.[142] Gordan is likely correct that being barred from this lecture was harmful for her career, or at minimum frustrated it, especially because it was purely on the grounds of sexism – she was a respected teacher and

---

[139] Lawrence, "Minutes of the Hroswitha Club," January 1974, n.p.

[140] Gordon, *Fifteenth-Century Books*.

[141] Lawrence, "Minutes of the Hroswitha Club," January 1974, n.p. The meeting minutes do not specify which event this was, but from looking through all possibly relevant Grolier exhibits in this period, this is the one that fits. The listed books are all in Howard Gordon's library, verified with Phyllis Gordan's checklist. As the prose shows, Bühler was a friend to the Goodhart family and would have been a natural choice for exhibition curator.

[142] Ong and Holzenberg, "Books of the First Half Century of Printing, 1450–1500," pp. 356–357.

scholar. In this respect, Bühler agreed with Gordan. In 1959, he published a biography in *Grolier 75* that praised Gordan's bibliographic work and argued that "it is a pity beyond measure that Howard Goodhart's only child is disqualified by her sex from full and active membership in the Club."[143]

Gordan's sentiments in conversation with Haight's are notable in that they reflect a dissonance in the club's membership in how to think about the Grolier Club's single-sex policies and the Hroswitha Club's relationship to them. Gordan does not disagree with Haight's claims that the Hroswitha Club did not need the Grolier Club to be legitimate, but because she has a career focused on her rare book expertise, not being allowed to attend the Grolier Club's events and network impacts her in a more distinct way. This sets up a dynamic of the feminized amateur in contrast to the masculinized professional, and professional women were caught in an uncomfortable in-betweenness. In her interview, Rebecca More noted that professional women would have always benefited more from the Grolier Club, which had ties to the institutions where these women worked and scholarly legitimacy, whether or not that was a fair or gendered distinction.

The Grolier Club began admitting women in 1976, bowing to social pressures, and a portion of the Hroswitha Club's membership was absorbed quickly. The first two women in the Grolier Club were Phyllis Gordan and Mary Hyde Eccles, followed shortly by Mary Massey and Mina Ruese Bryan, then Julia Wightman.[144] In a moment that perhaps exemplifies the "in-betweenness" of a new feminine working professional, Eccles and Goodhart's invitations to the Grolier Club were addressed to "Sir" with the apologies that

---

[143]   Bühler, *Grolier 75*, p. 220.

[144]   Abraham, "The Spirit of '76," p. 32. Abraham's article is a fascinating history about the Grolier's ideas about gender, which are complementary to this article's focus. Eccles later joined the Hroswitha Club in 1978 and was in Grolier Club first. This is a curious order of events, and my hypothesis is that she was happily absorbed in the Grolier Club's dealings and did not see a need to supplement them with membership in the Hroswitha Club – or she was not asked until the women mixed more within the Grolier Club.

they had not the time to print new ones with feminine honorifics.[145] In the announcement of new members in 1976 that Eccles kept in her papers, she has underlined every woman's name with a red pen, and she continued the practice of noting when women were invited to join the Grolier Club and attending those particular teas to meet them.[146]

It seems to be usually argued, by both historians and some Hroswithians, that the Grolier Club admitting women is what precipitated the end of the Hroswitha Club. This is certainly a factor as I outline previously, but I believe that a more nuanced account is needed that considers the wider social context of when the club declined and how its membership responded to this reality. In the 1980s and 1990s, the Hroswitha Club continued to position itself as a social club for amateurs, but this positioning began to lose its importance for women bibliophiles who had different opportunities available to them. In the 1950s, a collectors club provided a valuable vehicle for self-enrichment when women had fewer formal opportunities for education and employment. In the 1980s and 1990s, this was no longer true, and the club shifted more toward a leisure activity. Compared to the Grolier Club, which offered professional benefits and prestige from the beginning of its tenure, the latter became more attractive.

Accordingly, we see the following at the annual business meeting in 1988 when the group met, as they often did, in club president Julia Wightman's library, "where English oak paneling and shelves reached the ceiling were laden with bindings of morocco, mosaic, and mica."[147] In this familiar and serene space, Wightman dropped a "BOMBSHELL."

> IT seems to me that the HROSWITHA CLUB has served its purpose and its era, and it is time to disolve [sic] it under this name. It was formed by dedicated women collectors with outstanding Collections of books, and knowledge – to learn more about their libraries. Since the Grolier Club would not have them they formed their own Club, and

[145] The Grolier Club, Letter to Mrs. Donald Hyde, 1976.
[146] The Grolier Club, 1976. New Members in the Order of Their Election.
[147] Ashby, "Julia Parker Wightman," p. 391.

have carried on for 44 years, now we are graciously invited
to join the Grolier Club and talk books in endless delight. Is
there any reason to carry on our separate ways? Would it
not be better to bow out and all be bibliomaniacs
together?[148]

Wightman identifies three major reasons why the club needed to have this
discussion. First, they were "incorporated." That is, many Hroswithians
(including Wightman) were also in the Grolier Club, and a gendered divide
felt arbitrary. This was seconded by Susanna Borghese, who retrospectively
observed that by this period, there just were not that many women collectors who were not already in the Grolier Club. Secondly, the club was not as
active as many of its key members had passed away or resigned due to ill
health – Haight and Holden in 1977, Prescott in 1980, Stillwell and
Katharine Bull in 1984, Brown and Bryan in 1985, Marie Bullock in 1986,
and Troxell in 1987. Wightman's notes indicate that only six to eight of the
members attend meetings regularly.[149] Third, Wightman argues that "times
have changed" and "no one has time anymore." The club had shifted
toward vocational members, and it was much less common and socially
expected for women to stay home, meaning the logistics of running the club
without staff, as the Grolier Club had, made continuing unfeasible.

The Hroswitha Club members' responses are not recorded in
Wightman's notes, but there was an understanding that it would continue
though in an abbreviated fashion. Leadership wrote to members in 1990 that
they would cease collecting dues and limit meetings.[150] When Wightman
died in 1994, club engagement and attention to formal rules slipped as well.
The archives detail increasingly less attention to the structures of the early
days, which Deborah Evetts hypothesizes was reflective of losing their
longtime leader.[151] Wightman was passionate about books, wealthy, had
a beautiful library for meetings, and leisure time. No other Hroswithians

---

[148]　Wightman, "Hroswitha Club Meeting," January 1988, n.p.
[149]　Wightman, "Hroswitha Club Meeting," February 1990, n.p.
[150]　Wightman, "Hroswitha Club Meeting," 1990, n.p.
[151]　Evetts, Deborah 2022 pers. comm.

could fill such an important gap in the club. Illustratively, Elizabeth M. Riley, a former club officer, wrote to copresident Sarah Morgan in May 2001: "How do we elect members these days? Do you and Susanne [Borghese] decide it between you? Should the member be a collector? Are the other members notified? Have we any say in the matter?"[152] Morgan's response shows a still-active leadership that answered these questions quickly and thoroughly (she ponders a membership chair), but a general disconnect clearly remained.

In June 2003, Morgan and Borghese stepped down as copresidents.[153] No other member volunteered to replace them, so in 2004, they negotiated with the Grolier Club to take care of the Hroswitha Club's archives and offer blanket membership, at a reduced rate, to the remaining Hroswithians who were not already members.[154] In the Grolier Club's council meeting minutes, an unknown hand of a recording secretary writes that "Mr. [Donald] Orseman explained ... the original motivation for the Hroswitha Club evaporated when Grolier Club began to admit women as members."[155] Orseman's assessment seems to concur with Wightman's about the motivation for the club coming solely from not being allowed in the Grolier Club, which shows a shift in how to interpret this moment from Haight's point of view in the 1970s. While the "original motivation had evaporated," some other motivations kept women like Haight in the club – likely the very different nature of their gatherings and the kinship bonds they had formed and, perhaps, the knowledge that they accepted each other and made their own space for legitimacy and enrichment when others would not have them. The Grolier Club accepting women was certainly an important event, but it cannot be identified as the *only* reason the club folded. It seems more likely that when many of the original and key members had died, especially Wightman, *and* cultural shifts make it less likely for members to have time, the club's separateness became a burden

---

152 Riley, "Letter to Sarah Morgan," Mary 2001, n.p.
153 Morgan, "Memo from Sarah Morgan," September 2003, n.p.
154 Oresman, "Letter to Susanna [Mrs. Livio] Borghese," September 14, 2004, Box 2. Hroswitha Club Archive at the Grolier Club.
155 Unknown, "Transcription of Grolier Council Meeting Minutes," 2004.

rather than a benefit. The Grolier Club had a building with its library, staff, and prestige from association with masculinized knowledge; they had large fundraisers to support much of this work and publications. Where the Hroswitha Club is rarely mentioned in a member's obituary, membership in the Grolier Club is readily and often pointed to as a symbol of a deceased member's excellence. For members that were concerned with their professional responsibilities, there seem to be a clear way forward. Similarly to the absorption of Barnard College into Columbia and Radcliffe College into Harvard, the Hroswitha Club was absorbed into the Grolier Club.

Coda: Book Collecting, Literary History, and Women's Labor

This narrative has, I hope, made visible the extent to which members of the Hroswitha Club have impacted the study of rare books and artifacts. Some of these collections are impressive enough to have always garnered attention; certainly, the Hyde collection at the Houghton (which supported this work), Dumbarton Oaks, and the Hunt Institute are names familiar to scholars in the fields who use these objects and artifacts. Taken collectively, however, the reach of this group's collections should make a strong case for their significance beyond Wikipedia, in the study of rare books in the United States.

While completing this project, I circled around a particular point without satisfactorily resolving it: why wasn't this story told before? Many of these women have power, privilege, and institutional access limited to only the most well-connected of women in this period. The original members were participants in the Golden Age of collecting, when US institutions and private collectors with deep pockets rapidly purchased rare materials and cultural artifacts from other countries such as Great Britain.[156] For a number of them, the only barrier to the renown given to their male contemporaries (and relatives) like Lewis, Rosenbach, Huntington, Houghton, and Morgan was gender norms, many of which shifted even during these women's lives.

But while I grappled with this nagging question of absences in the wider discussion of collecting and rare books, I realized I was positioning this incorrectly. This story *had* been told before. It was told by the women themselves, carefully and meticulously over a half a century. It was told through newspaper clippings, handwritten invitations, meeting minutes detailing exhibits and lectures manually copied on typewriters, thank-you notes in the mail, and publications by the Hroswitha Club, with their name proudly on the cover. Members and appointed librarians organized the club's documents, and routinely returned to these archives to ensure they had a copy of all the minutes. The archive was discussed over years in the minutes, as it and the library found several new homes before arriving at the

---

[156] Chen, *Placing Papers*, ch.1, Rosenbach, "Why America Buys England's Books," and Tamarkin.

Grolier Club in 2004. Then, the Grolier Club's librarians and catalogers processed the material, wrote the finding aid and allowed researchers like me to use these documents. Through the narrative I have woven from this archive and supplemental research is a story of not just what the club did and who they were, but the traces of women's hands who ensured that their story would survive beyond their organization. This was never a "lost" story; what has changed with this Element is simply the audience and format.

I hope that this project is a step forward in the process of recovering and making visible the ways that women collectors have participated in the study of rare books in the United States. We have long recognized the amateur gentleman collector as an object of fascination, and it is time that women are at least acknowledged among them, but beyond that these women should help us ask new questions of what histories, labor, and resources support our study. Scholars routinely use Hroswithians' books and travel with funds from their donated fortunes, and it is essential that we name their contributions and begin to name that of so many others. This would be a profound legacy for them, indeed.

Appendix: Club Membership 1944–1994

This list represents the Hroswitha Club membership from 1944 to 1994. A final membership list given to the Grolier Club by Sarah Morgan or Susanna Borghese in early 2005 provided the end dates for many of the later members.[1]

The appendix uses a taxonomy designed to differentiate transcriptions from researched information. There are three largely transcribed categories: Formal Name, Membership Years, and Collection Focus or Expertise. Formal names are pulled verbatim from club records, typically within formally printed membership lists. When a member changed names through marriage or divorce, multiple formal names are recorded. The 1994 omnibus membership list is the most thorough, but as it is not without errors, dates and typos to names are changed using other records. Most members were members until their deaths, occasionally stepping down to associates when health, distance, or other concerns prevented them from attending meetings or other activities. Some were promoted to honorary. Collection foci are paraphrased and quoted from membership lists, sometimes combined across versions, with changes to mechanics to make the list consistent. I also added full author names and corrected clear typos in names of books.

Two categories are researched: the full name that begins each entry and Repositories and Associations. Full names were researched by the author with significant assistance from the listserv for the Society of the History of Authorship, Reading, and Publishing, the Ex-Libris listserv, and friends in the rare book community. Names with [brackets] are not 100 percent confirmed but are likely based on outside research and club records. Nicknames, marked with "quotes," were retained so those accessing archival records can be sure of identification. Repositories and Associations was compiled through a combination of references in membership lists, meeting minutes, and outside research using WorldCat, the Social Networks and Archival Context Cooperative, ArchiveGrid, and search engines. An institution

---

[1] Unknown, "Membership List," April 25, 2005.

was added if it contained listed references to the subject's name, including formerly owned artifacts, related correspondence, and other documents. I also added institutions if the subject worked there and their labor would be represented in the institution's catalog, finding aids, collections, or the like, even if it is unsigned. Given the large social networks of these members, we limited listed institutions to ones that hold books or other rare artifacts and special collections. Obituaries for the members, usually accessible with a search engine and full names, often list the other organizations these women belonged to. This list is unlikely to be comprehensive given the scattered nature of metadata and the prevalence of unsigned labor, but it represents a starting place for future research and a way to map the impact of these collectors, catalogers, and librarians.

Hroswitha Club Membership, 1944–1994

[Josephine F.] Baker

Formal Name: Mrs. Daniel Baker, Jr.

Membership Years: 1961–89

Collection Focus/Expertise: Books with fore-edge paintings

Repositories and Associations: Unknown

Marjorie Dana Barlow

Formal Name: Mrs. William Tait Barlow

Membership Years: 1944–85

Collection Focus/Expertise: Boxiana; William Hazlitt; women printers in the United States

Repositories and Associations: The Grolier Club

Marjorie Young Gibbon Battles

Formal Name: Mrs. Winthrop H. Battles

Membership Years: 1962–99

Collection Focus/Expertise: Herbals and seventeenth- and eighteenth-century French plays

Repositories and Associations: Historical Society of Pennsylvania

Henrietta Collins Bartlett

Formal Name: Miss Bartlett

Membership Years: 1944–63

Collection Focus/Expertise: Bibliography reference books and English books before 1700

Repositories and Associations: Beinecke Library, Yale University

Frances Kennedy Black

Formal Name: Mrs. Corwin Black

Membership Years: 1964–93

Collection Focus/Expertise: Books on travel, especially early travelers and excavations; Byzantine Empire and early Christianity

Repositories and Associations: New York Public Library; Morgan Library & Museum

Mildred Barnes Bliss

Formal Name: Mrs. Robert W. Bliss

Membership Years: 1953–69

Collection Focus/Expertise: Association Library; Garden Library at Dumbarton Oaks, Washington, DC

Repositories and Associations: Dumbarton Oaks, Harvard University

Ruth Frankel Boorstin

Formal Name: Mrs. Daniel J. Boorstin

Membership Years: 1977–2004

Collection Focus/Expertise: Libraries; the history of painting; Renaissance literature

Repositories and Associations: Library of Congress

Susanna "Saz" Borghese

Formal Name: Mrs. Livio Borghese

Membership Years: 1990–2004

Collection Focus/Expertise: Miniature books; vellum bindings; books on historical or contemporary bindings or binders; trade bindings 1890–1930; artist's books

Repositories and Associations: The Grolier Club; some still in collector's hands

Alice Brayton

Formal Name: Miss Brayton

Membership Years: 1944–72

Collection Focus/Expertise: Rhode Island history, George Berkeley, and "books that are a lot more interesting"

Repositories and Associations: John Hay Library, Brown University; Green Animals Topiary Garden

Anne Seddon Kinsolving Brown

Formal Name: Mrs. John Nichols Brown

Membership Years: 1949–85

Collection Focus/Expertise: Illustrated books on military history

Repositories and Associations: John Hay Library, Brown University

Mina Ruese Bryan

Formal Name: Mrs. Samuel S. Bryan, Jr.

Membership Years: 1968–85

Collection Focus/Expertise: Incunabula and early manuscripts, voyages, Americana; books and manuscripts relating to the Americans in Paris in the 1920s

Repositories and Associations: Princeton University Library

Katharine "Paddy" Davis Exton Bull

Formal Name: Mrs. Ludlow Bull

Membership Years: 1951–84

Collection Focus/Expertise: Bookbinding, embroidery, and books pertaining to these subjects

Repositories and Associations: Princeton University Library

Marie Leontine Graves Bullock

Formal Name: Mrs. Hugh Bullock

Membership Years: 1951–86

Collection Focus/Expertise: Inscribed first editions of poetry; William Blake drawings; fore-edge paintings; astronomical and scientific books

Repositories and Associations: Academy of American Poets

Eleanor Towne Carey

Formal Name: Mrs. W. Gibson Carey

Membership Years: 1971–2

Collection Focus/Expertise: English history, archaeology, early medieval architecture, and sculpture

Repositories and Associations: Reported that collection dispersed to family; one book donated to Morgan Library & Museum

Rachel Caruthers

Formal Name: Miss Caruthers

Membership Years: 1950–8

Collection Focus/Expertise: Plays and books pertaining to the stage

Repositories and Associations: Unknown

Beatrice "Happy" Oenslager Chace

Formal Name: Mrs. Malcolm G. Chace, Jr.

Membership Years: 1963–92

Collection Focus/Expertise: Americana and restoration of old houses; first editions of American authors; Willa Cather, Ernest Hemingway, and William Faulkner

Repositories and Associations: Smith College Special Collections

[Barbara Vaughn Bail] Collins

Formal Name: Mrs. Frederick A. Collins, Jr.

Membership Years: 1952–?

Collection Focus/Expertise: Jane Austen and Henry Handel Richardson

Repositories and Associations: Unknown

Mabel Choate

Formal Name: Miss Choate

Membership Years: 1944–58

Collection Focus/Expertise: Books on modern painters – Monet, Manet, Picasso, Matisse, and so on; also books on New England

Repositories and Associations: Archives and Research Center, The Trustees; New York Botanical Garden

Armida Maria-Theresa Colt

Formal Name: Mrs. H. Dunscombe Colt

Membership Years: 1983–2004

Collection Focus/Expertise: Festival books; preservation of old houses; small private presses

Repositories and Associations: Library of Congress

[Margaret Hillsdale] Crosby

Formal Name: Mrs. Everett U. Crosby

Membership Years: 1951–3

Collection Focus/Expertise: First editions of Charles Lamb, both English and American; scattered first editions of E. V. Lucas, John Masefield, Joseph Conrad, A. Edward Newton, and some modern American poets

Repositories and Associations: Unknown

Barbara "Babs" Clay Debevoise

Formal Name: Mrs. Clay Debevoise

Membership Years: 1965–90

Collection Focus/Expertise: Ancient civilization, especially the Middle East, Sumer; working library on the History of Art

Repositories and Associations: Ex-husband's papers are at Amherst College

Clelia C. Benjamin Delafield

Formal Name: Mrs. Edward C. Delafield

Membership Years: 1956–74

Collection Focus/Expertise: Orchids; books on birds, flowers, and related subjects

Repositories and Associations: Unknown

Violetta Susan Elizabeth White Delafield

Formal Name: Mrs. John Ross Delafield

Membership Years: 1947–9

Collection Focus/Expertise: Early works on American flora and botany or books relating to the flower arrangements; flower lore and symbolism; interesting bindings of the period of publication

Repositories and Associations: New York Public Library; Bard College

Catherine Dunscomb Colt Dickey

Formal Name: Mrs. Charles D. Dickey, Jr.

Membership Years: 1944–73

Collection Focus/Expertise: Illustrated natural history books; eighteenth and nineteenth centuries, principally birds and butterflies; Hudson River books, maps, and prints; children's books

Repositories and Associations: Reported that collection dispersed to family

Margaret Bell Douglas

Formal Name: Mrs. Walter Douglas

Membership Years: 1944–63

Collection Focus/Expertise: Gardening, architecture, voyages, oriental paintings and prints, old silver; a few editions of Rudyard Kipling and Charles Dickens

Repositories and Associations: Desert Botanical Garden in Phoenix, Arizona

Frances Converse Massey Dulaney

Formal Name: Mrs. Edward E. Dulaney

Membership Years: 1976–2004

Collection Focus/Expertise: Edward Gorey; nineteenth- and twentieth-century children's books on pigs and illustrated children's book; the British royal family from Edward VII to the present; Arthur Rackham

Repositories and Associations: Still in collector's hands

Alice Fellowes Stowell Durant

Formal Name: Mrs. Donald Durant

Membership Years: 1944–60

Collection Focus/Expertise: Floral and fruit prints of the seventeenth, eighteenth, and nineteenth centuries; illustrated gardening and botanical books, herbals, books on roses; early nineteenth-century small books; colored floral and fruit illustrations; books, prints, and maps of the Hudson River

Repositories and Associations: Horticultural Society of New York; New-York Historical Society; Library of the Garden Club of America

Mary Crapo Hyde Eccles

Formal Name: Mrs. Donald Hyde; Viscountess Eccles

Membership Years: 1978–?

Collection Focus/Expertise: Eighteenth-century England: particularly Samuel Johnson, James Boswell, Mrs. Hester Thrale, and Henry Fielding; nineteenth century: Oscar Wilde, Norman Douglas, and George Bernard Shaw; British coronation material and forgeries of William Henry Ireland; Japanese literacy manuscripts and history of Japanese printing

Repositories and Associations: Houghton Library, Harvard University; British Library; New York Public Library; The Grolier Club; Morgan Library & Museum; Two River Farm

Emily Gildersleeve English

Formal Name: Mrs. Robert B. English

Membership Years: 1944–74

Collection Focus/Expertise: Plant illustration; nineteenth- and twentieth-century garden books; books of exploration and travel; foreign botanists in the United States

Repositories and Associations: Unknown

Deborah H. Evetts

Formal Name: Miss Evetts

Membership Years: 1980–2004

Collection Focus/Expertise: Find bindings; conservation; decorated book papers; miniature books and bindings

Repositories and Associations: The Hroswitha Club Archive, The Grolier Club; Morgan Library & Museum

Gertrude Helen Schirmer Fay

Formal Name: Mrs. William R. Fay

Membership Years: 1959–1990

Collection Focus/Expertise: Out-of-print and unusual travel books; poetry and poetry anthologies; foreign illustrated children's books, illuminated manuscripts, and ancient printed books that have been acquired in course of travel during the last decade

Repositories and Associations: Northeast Harbor Library; Houghton Library, Harvard University

Sarah Gildersleeve Fife

Formal Name: Mrs. Robert Herndon Fife

Membership Years: 1944–9

Collection Focus/Expertise: Botanical works with plates from 1700; books of travel and exploration, particularly by botanists

Repositories and Associations: New York Botanical Garden; The Hroswitha Club Archive, The Grolier Club

Elizabeth "Betty" Carson Fox

Formal Name: Mrs. William Logan Fox

Membership Years: 1949–74

Collection Focus/Expertise: Americana; books about books

Repositories and Associations: Morgan Library & Museum

Alice Knotts Bossert Cooney Frelinghuysen

Formal Name: Mrs. George L. K. Frelinghuysen

Membership Years: 1986–2004

Collection Focus/Expertise: Working library of nineteenth- and twentieth-century books on ceramics and glass; illustrated garden books of the Edwardian period; first editions of Edith Wharton

Repositories and Associations: The Met

Elizabeth van Cortlandt Lyman Frelinghuysen

Formal Name: Mrs. Frederick Frelinghuysen

Membership Years: 1975–83

Collection Focus/Expertise: History; social history; nineteenth-century libraries; memoirs

Repositories and Associations: Gunston Hall Library; New Jersey Historical Society; reported that family received papers and collection

Phyllis Walter Goodhart Gordan

Formal Name: Mrs. John D. Gordan

Membership Years: 1960–94

Collection Focus/Expertise: Incunabula; humanist literature and history of the fifteenth century; Medieval Latin

Repositories and Associations: Bryn Mawr

Ruth Shepard Granniss

Formal Name: Miss Granniss

Membership Years: 1944–54

Collection Focus/Expertise: Stamped Victorian bindings; Librarian and Curator of The Grolier Club

Repositories and Associations: The Grolier Club; Columbia University Library; Houghton Library, Harvard University

Belle da Costa Greene

Formal Name: Miss Greene

Membership Years: 1944–1950

Collection Focus/Expertise: Director, The Pierpont Morgan Library

Repositories and Associations: Morgan Library & Museum; reportedly given to Anne Haight

Anne Lyon Haight

Formal Name: Mrs. Sherman Post Haight

Membership Years: 1944–77

Collection Focus/Expertise: Early English literature and children's books; print history, including George Cruikshank; William Makepeace Thackeray

Repositories and Associations: New-York Historical Society; Morgan Library & Museum; Trinity College Library

Meta Harrsen

Formal Name: Miss Harrsen

Membership Years: 1958–1977

Collection Focus/Expertise: Author of books and articles on medieval manuscripts, including the Nekcsei-Lipocz Bible, published by the Library of Congress in 1949; Fulbright grants for research in Europe 1951 and 1955; Keeper of Manuscripts, the Pierpont Morgan Library to 1958

Repositories and Associations: Morgan Library & Museum

Iola Stetson Haverstick

Formal Name: Mrs. Iola S. Haverstick

Membership Years: 1980–?

Collection Focus/Expertise: Eighteenth- and nineteenth-century English and American literature, particularly Henry James and Edith Wharton

Repositories and Associations: Barnard College, Columbia University; Yale Center for British Art

Agnes MacArthur Hayes

Formal Name: Mrs. Sadler Hayes

Membership Years: 1980–?

Collection Focus/Expertise: Thomas Wolfe; eighteenth-century English and American antiques

Repositories and Associations: Davidson College Archives and Special Collections

Caroline Herod

Formal Name: Mrs. William Rogers Herod

Membership Years: 1985–?

Collection Focus/Expertise: Music, music as therapy; prehistory, archaeology; theology; historic biographies; world affairs

Repositories and Associations: Morgan Library & Museum

Chantal S. Leroy Hodges

Formal Name: Mrs. Fletcher Hodges III

Membership Years: 1977–2004

Collection Focus/Expertise: Children's books and illustrated books circa 1850–1950; preference for fantasy and fairy, first editions of classics, and autographed books; limited editions

Repositories and Associations: Northeast Historic Film; Oxford University Press

Miriam Young Holden

Formal Name: Mrs. Arthur C. Holden

Membership Years: 1957–77

Collection Focus/Expertise: Books revealing women's roles in civilization, their political, legal, and economic status, and their progress in education, science, culture, and religions, from primitive times to the present

Repositories and Associations: Princeton Rare Books and Manuscripts; Firestone Library, Princeton

Frances Milliken Hooper

Formal Name: Miss Frances Hooper

Membership Years: 1965–86

Collection Focus/Expertise: Kate Greenaway: original watercolors, first editions, manuscripts, letters, articles, and pamphlets about her, and books she has reviewed; Laurence Sterne; illustrated editions of *Sentimental Journey*

Repositories and Associations: Hunt Institute, Carnegie Mellon University; Chicago Horticultural Society; Smith College Special Collections; Duke University; University of Chicago

Jane Wild Howe

Formal Name: Mrs. Walter Howe

Membership Years: 1951–2004

Collection Focus/Expertise: Seventeenth- and early eighteenth-century English literature; reports to the Royal Society and courtesy books of the same period; James Stephens and the Irish Renaissance writers

Repositories and Associations: Unknown

Hannah Johnson Howell

Formal Name: Mrs. Henry W. Howell, Jr.

Membership Years: 1970–88

Collection Focus/Expertise: Medieval art; archaeology; Romanesque sculpture and travel

Repositories and Associations: Frick Collection

Rachel McMasters Miller Hunt

Formal Name: Mrs. Roy Arthur Hunt

Membership Years: 1944–63

Collection Focus/Expertise: Herbals, gardening books, travel literature, and private presses; bindings and book plates; portraits and autographs of botanists

Repositories and Associations: Hunt Institute, Carnegie Mellon University; Roy A. Hunt Foundation

Margaret Urling Sibley Iselin

Formal Name: Mrs. O'Donnell Iselin

Membership Years: 1946–51

Collection Focus/Expertise: First editions of children's books; Mark Twain, Kipling, Howard Pyle, and so on. First editions of some modern authors such as E. M. Foster, Virginia Woolf, Sherwood Anderson, and D. H. Lawrence

Repositories and Associations: Reported that it was sold to benefit St. Timothy's School, Maryland; Sibley Watson Digital Archive

Suzanne Fonay Wemple

Formal Name: Dr. Suzanne Fonay Kindred

Membership Years: 1982–2004

Collection Focus/Expertise: American and English authors on women in European history, especially medieval

Repositories and Associations: Barnard College, Columbia University

Miriam Boothby Lawrence

Formal Name: Mrs. George H. M. Lawrence; Mrs. M. B. Lawrence

Membership Years: 1970–84

Collection Focus/Expertise: Bookbinding; American miniature books

Repositories and Associations: Husband's papers are at the University of Rhode Island Library

Mary S. Leahy

Formal Name: Mrs. John Jay Leahy

Membership Years: 1983–2004

Collection Focus/Expertise: Books on or about Mary Cassatt

Repositories and Associations: Bryn Mawr

Anne Burr Auchincloss Lewis

Formal Name: Mrs. Wilmarth S. Lewis

Membership Years: 1948–59

Collection Focus/Expertise: Curator of Lewis collection of eighteenth-century political and satirical prints at the Yale Walpole library

Repositories and Associations: Lewis Walpole Library, Yale University

Sarah Larkin Loening

Formal Name: Mrs. Albert P. Loening

Membership Years: 1946–88

Collection Focus/Expertise: Early Canadiana; books on bees

Repositories and Associations: Unknown

Rosamond Bowditch Loring

Formal Name: Mrs. Augustus P. Loring

Membership Years: 1944–50

Collection Focus/Expertise: Decorated book papers; juvenile books; Horace Walpole's Strawberry Hill Press; paper bindings

Repositories and Associations: Houghton Library, Harvard University; the Club of Odd Volumes

Eleanor Cross Marquand

Formal Name: Mrs. Allan Marquand

Membership Years: 1944–50

Collection Focus/Expertise: Books on early botany; books on history of symbolism through the Renaissance; collection presented to the Library of the New York Botanical Gardens

Repositories and Associations: New York Botanical Garden

Louise Scheide Marshall

Formal Name: Mrs. Gordon M. Marshall, Jr.

Membership Years: 1972–84

Collection Focus/Expertise: Laws and early histories of the American Colonies; eighteenth- and nineteenth-century political thought

Repositories and Associations: Library Company; American Antiquarian Society; still in collector's hands

Mary Ord Preston Massey

Formal Name: Mrs. Linton R. Massey

Membership Years: 1962–2004

Collection Focus/Expertise: Herbals from the fifteenth century to the present day; early American botanists and garden books

Repositories and Associations: Folger Shakespeare Library; University of Virginia

Lily Lambert McCarthy

Formal Name: Mrs. John Gilman McCarthy

Membership Years: 1955–2004

Collection Focus/Expertise: Book bindings; miniature books; Lord Nelson and books pertaining to him

Repositories and Associations: Portsmouth Central Library

Mary Tyler Freeman Cheek McClenahan

Formal Name: Mrs. Leslie Cheek, Jr.; Mrs. John L. McClannahan [*sic*]

Membership Years: 1981–2004

Collection Focus/Expertise: Southern American women, a complete collection of Ellen Glasgow, now working on first editions of her works; the Library of Douglas S. Freeman autographed

Repositories and Associations: Virginia Commonwealth University

Martha Harding Bakewell McKnight

Formal Name: Mrs. Thomas Harden Baird McKnight

Membership Years: 1948–1962

Collection Focus/Expertise: Biography; letters and collections of books on World War II; biography and letters of Civil War

Repositories and Associations: University of Pittsburgh; Senator John Heinz History Center, The Pennsylvania State University

Elinor Gregory Metcalf

Formal Name: Mrs. K. D. Metcalf

Membership Years: 1944–7

Collection Focus/Expertise: Library of the Boston Athenaeum

Repositories and Associations: Boston Athenaeum

Agnes Malcolm Gayley Milliken

Formal Name: Mrs. Gerrish H. Milliken

Membership Years: 1944–64

Collection Focus/Expertise: William Blake; Greek literature; William Shakespeare; eighteenth-century letters; garden books

Repositories and Associations: Northeast Harbor Library; Southwest Harbor Public Library; University of California at Berkeley

Katherine "Kay" Curstin Miller

Formal Name: Mrs. Sidney T. Miller

Membership Years: 1961–?

Collection Focus/Expertise: Incunabula; fine printing; early exploration, especially concerning Michigan, the artic, and Northwest territory

Repositories and Associations: Partially sold through Sotheby's in 2014; Incunabula Short Title Catalog lists provenance for six books to Mrs. Miller

Dorothy Miner

Formal Name: Miss Miner

Membership Years: 1954–73

Collection Focus/Expertise: Medieval illuminated manuscripts; incunabula; early printing and illustrations; book bindings

Repositories and Associations: Walters Art Gallery and Maryland Institute, College of Art Library

Rebecca Weeks Sherrill More

Formal Name: Mrs. Timothy T. More

Membership Years: 1971–2004

Collection Focus/Expertise: French cookbooks; working library of cook and gastric books; books relating to eighteenth-century colonial architecture

Repositories and Associations: Brown University; still in collector's hands

Sarah "Sally" Baldwin Lambert Morgan

Formal Name: Mrs. Charles F. Morgan

Membership Years: 1991–2004

Collection Focus/Expertise: English literature and angling books seventeenth, eighteenth, and nineteenth centuries; natural history nineteenth century (some Thomas Bewick books and engravings); American angling nineteenth and twentieth centuries; English drawings, watercolors eighteenth and nineteenth centuries

Repositories and Associations: Unknown

Katharine "Kay" Starr Oliver

Formal Name: Mrs. Peter Oliver

Membership Years: 1964–81

Collection Focus/Expertise: Horace, botanical illustrated books; *Compleat Angler*

Repositories and Associations: Middletown College has a book fund in her name

Catharine Tinker Patterson

Formal Name: Mrs. George Patterson

Membership Years: 1950–63

Collection Focus/Expertise: Italian and Spanish art; modern children's literature; drawings, first editions, letters and manuscripts of Walter Crane, and original books made for his own children

Repositories and Associations: Beinecke Library and Sterling Library, Yale University; Blanton Museum of Art

Clara Sargent Peck

Formal Name: Miss Peck

Membership Years: 1954–1983

Collection Focus/Expertise: Books and manuscripts on various sporting subjects from many countries and Natural History

Repositories and Associations: Transylvania University; Corning Museum of Glass; Rockwell Museum; Princeton University Art Museum; Morgan Library & Museum

Deirdre Howard Pirie

Formal Name: Mrs. Robert S. Pirie

Membership Years: 1982–2004

Collection Focus/Expertise: Antelope books; coaching and other equestrian books; cookery

Repositories and Associations: Some of collection sold through Robin Bledsoe in 2017; ex-husband's papers are at the Grolier Club

Marjorie Wiggin Prescott

Formal Name: Mrs. Sherburne Prescott

Membership Years: 1946–80

Collection Focus/Expertise: First editions of English and American literature with manuscript tie-ins, including Rudyard Kipling, Samuel
Johnson, and Charles Dickens

Repositories and Associations: Sold through Christie's in the "Prescott
Collection" in 1981; The Grolier Club

Jane Quinby

Formal Name: Miss Jane Quinby

Membership Years: 1954–65

Collection Focus/Expertise: Contemporary first editions and manuscripts;
Beatrix Potter, Tasha Tudor, biography, travel, and literature in the
tenth century

Repositories and Associations: Hunt Institute, Carnegie Mellon University

Elizabeth "Liz" Mildred Riley

Formal Name: Miss Elizabeth Riley

Membership Years: 1976–2002

Collection Focus/Expertise: Needlework bindings; working libraries on
Far Eastern arts, particularly textiles; twentieth-century poetry; lady
detective story writers; Anthony Trollope

Repositories and Associations: Cooper Hewitt, Smithsonian; Metropolitan
Museum of Art; Morgan Library & Museum

[Gladis] Robinson

Formal Name: Mrs. Beverley R. Robinson

Membership Years: 1944–72

Collection Focus/Expertise: Books on London

Repositories and Associations: Reported that collection was sold according
to her will

Edith Goodkind Rosenwald

Formal Name: Mrs. Lessing J. Rosenwald

Membership Years: 1957–92

Collection Focus/Expertise: English and American first editions of
A. A. Milne and other children's books.

Repositories and Associations: Library of Congress; National Gallery of Art

Elizabeth E. Roth

Formal Name: Miss Roth

Membership Years: 1975–2004

Collection Focus/Expertise: Prints and drawings; illustrated books and fine bindings

Repositories and Associations: New York Public Library; Getty Research Institute

Janet Lindsay Burns Saint-Germain

Formal Name: Mrs. Peter M. Saint-Germain

Membership Years: 1984–2004

Collection Focus/Expertise: Restoration; hand-bookbinding; Scottish literature and history; particularly the poems and songs of Robert Byrne

Repositories and Associations: Innerpeffray Library in Scotland

[Jane Bell Yeatman] Savage

Formal Name: Mrs. Ernest C. Savage

Membership Years: 1962–?

Collection Focus/Expertise: Books on art (mostly Renaissance), archeology, travel, gardens, china, silver, and furniture

Repositories and Associations: Unknown

Notes: I am relatively certain this is Jane Bell Yeatman and not Sarah Trowbridge, Jane's daughter-in-law, given that the 1964 and 1970 membership lists have an address in the Chestnut Hill neighborhood of Pennsylvania; however, Ernest Chauncy Savage and his son Ernest Chauncy Savage, Jr. have demonstrably similar names, so I have kept the brackets

[Eleanor] Russell Scott

Formal Name: Mrs. Russell Scott

Membership Years: 1944–62

Collection Focus/Expertise: Books about saints; Egypt; travel

Repositories and Associations: Reportedly in the Hroswitha Library, The Grolier Club

Louise Elkins Sinkler

Formal Name: Mrs. Wharton Sinkler

Membership Years: 1944–77

Collection Focus/Expertise: Fine bird books from 1700; first editions of American books, prose, poetry, natural history exploration; working library on fine arts, silver, china, glass, and furniture

Repositories and Associations: Library Company; Springfield Township Historical Society; University of Pennsylvania

Bertha Coolidge Slade

Formal Name: Mrs. Marshall P. Slade

Membership Years: 1944–53

Collection Focus/Expertise: Maria Edgeworth; George Meredith; John Leech; Edward Lear; caricatures; Constance Holme; Lewis Carroll; eighteenth-century illustrated French books; signed eighteenth-century French bindings

Repositories and Associations: Beinecke Library, Yale University

Sharyl G. Smith

Formal Name: Miss Sharyl G. Smith

Membership Years: 1983–?

Collection Focus/Expertise: Children's books and reference books about books for children, specifically nursery rhyme books, ABC books, and twentieth-century American and European picture books for the young; posters that publicize children's literature or special collections of children's books

Repositories and Associations: still in collector's hands

Harriet Chapman Sprague

Formal Name: Mrs. Frank Sprague

Membership Years: 1944–69

Collection Focus/Expertise: Walt Whitman, American and English first editions; Bartlett's *Familiar Quotations*, all editions; Oliver Herford; Gelett Burgess; Stephen Crane, Bret Harte

Repositories and Associations: University of Pennsylvania; Chapin Library at Williams College; Trinity College Hartford

Helene Coughlin Sprague

Formal Name: Mrs. Julian K. Sprague

Membership Years: 1946–71

Collection Focus/Expertise: First editions of American authors, especially Mark Twain, Walt Whitman, Nathaniel Hawthorne, Ralph Waldo Emerson, Henry David Thoreau, Stephen Crane, and Lewis Carroll

Repositories and Associations: reportedly given to son Peter Sprague

Florence Antoinette van Zelm Sprague

Formal Name: Mrs. Robert C. Sprague

Membership Years: 1951–87

Collection Focus/Expertise: Willa Cather; Robert Frost; Sarah Orne Jewett; Edward Arlington Robinson; collection of Dorothy Doughty's birds and other ceramics

Repositories and Associations: Family company newsletters are at Freel Library, Massachusetts College of Liberal Arts

Margaret Bingham Stillwell

Formal Name: Miss Stillwell

Membership Years: 1950–84

Collection Focus/Expertise: Incunabula; Chinese art; scientific books of the fifteenth and sixteenth centuries

Repositories and Associations: John Hay Library and Annmary Brown Memorial, Brown University

May Margaret Egan Stokes

Formal Name: Mrs. J. Stogdell Stokes

Membership Years: 1961–76

Collection Focus/Expertise: The iconography of The Three Kings, especially in French Romanesque sculpture; working library, including photographs and varied illustrations

Repositories and Associations: Bryn Mawr; Philadelphia Museum of Art

[Mary Holbrook Wilson] Strong

Formal Name: Mrs. Austin Strong

Membership Years: 1949–68

Collection Focus/Expertise: Books, books, books
Repositories and Associations: Unknown

Lola Leontin Szladits

Formal Name: Dr. Lola L. Szladits
Membership Years: 1975–90
Collection Focus/Expertise: English and American literature, books and authors' manuscripts; drawings, mostly Dutch seventeenth century and Italian Renaissance
Repositories and Associations: The Grolier Club; New York Public Library

Lillian Gary Taylor

Formal Name: Mrs. Robert Coleman Taylor
Membership Years: 1946–61
Collection Focus/Expertise: "Outstanding" books in American fiction, first editions in original bindings
Repositories and Associations: Albert and Shirley Small Special Collections Library, University of Virginia

Helen Malarkey Thompson

Formal Name: Mrs. Stephen Eberly Thompson
Membership Years: 1966–?
Collection Focus/Expertise: Collection of fifteenth-century manuscripts of the "Horace Beatae Virginia Marie"; Geoffrey Chaucer, William Caxton, and Kelmscott Press
Repositories and Associations: John Wilson Special Collections, Multnomah County Library

Frances McKee Tinker

Formal Name: Mrs. Edward Laroque Tinker
Membership Years: 1953–8
Collection Focus/Expertise: General collection of English literature
Repositories and Associations: Harry Ransom Center, University of Texas

Mary Barker Treide

Formal Name: Mrs. Henry Ernest Treide
Membership Years: 1946–69

Collection Focus/Expertise: Early printing and merchant adventures

Repositories and Associations: Husband's papers are at the Baltimore Museum of Art

Janet Camp Troxell

Formal Name: Mrs. Gilbert Troxell

Membership Years: 1946–87

Collection Focus/Expertise: D. G. and Christina Rossetti; Pre-Raphaelites; Queen Victoria

Repositories and Associations: Rare Books and Manuscripts, Princeton University

Lila Ross Hotz Luce Tyng

Formal Name: Mrs. Lila Tyng

Membership Years: 1972–99

Collection Focus/Expertise: Poetry, first editions of nineteenth-century literature; miniature books

Repositories and Associations: Arthur and Elizabeth Schlesinger Library, Harvard University; Cooper Hewitt, Smithsonian

Anne Duff Macbeth Von Moschzisker

Formal Name: Mrs. Robert Von Moschzisker

Membership Years: 1944–50

Collection Focus/Expertise: Robert Frost; Charles Godfrey Leland; American and English first editions

Repositories and Associations: Amherst College

Janetta Alexander Whitridge

Formal Name: Mrs. Arnold Whitridge

Membership Years: 1963–73

Collection Focus/Expertise: Books on travelers to America from England and France between the years 1776 and 1860

Repositories and Associations: Beinecke Library, Yale University; New York Public Library

Julia Parker Wightman

Formal Name: Miss Wightman

Membership Years: 1955–94

Collection Focus/Expertise: Books on books, children's books, flower books, horse books, Aesop, emblem books, miniature books, and science fiction

Repositories and Associations: Morgan Library & Museum; New-York Historical Society; The Hroswitha Club Archive, The Grolier Club

Marian Hillyer Wolff Young

Formal Name: Mrs. John M. Young

Membership Years: 1975–2004

Collection Focus/Expertise: Historic preservation and great houses, Stratford Hall, Gunston Hall; complete collection of Lonsdale Library of Sports, Games and Pastimes; collection of Badminton Library of Sports; nineteenth-century authors: Anthony Trollope, Honoré de Balzac, Thomas Hardy, twentieth-century Thomas Mann

Repositories and Associations: Unknown

Mabel A. Zahn

Formal Name: Miss Zahn

Membership Years: 1968–74

Collection Focus/Expertise: Important Americana; first editions of nineteenth-century novels; rare prints; historical manuscripts

Repositories and Associations: Sessler's Bookshop (now closed)

Bibliography

Abraham, Mildred. 2001. "The Spirit of '76: The First Women of the Grolier Club." *Gazette of the Grolier Club*, New Series, 52: 31–47.

———. 2006. "Ruth Shepard Grannis (1872–1954), Grolier Librarian, Scholar, & Lecturer: A Truly Remarkable Woman." *Gazette of the Grolier Club*, New Series, no. 57: 24–49.

Abraham Simon Wolf Rosenbach. 1952. *Proceedings of the American Antiquarian Society*. *American Antiquarian Society*, October, 113–117.

Anonymous. 2020. "Rachel McMasters Miller Hunt: Plantswoman, Bookwoman, Craftswoman." Carnegie Mellon University Libraries. https://library.cmu.edu/about/news/2020-11/rachel-mcmasters-miller-hunt-plantswoman-bookwoman-craftswoman.

Archive of California. n.d. "Finding Aid to the Lois Rather Papers, circa 1877–1996 (Bulk 1945–1985)." https://oac.cdlib.org/findaid/ark:/13030/c8833t1j/.

Archives at the LuEsther T. Mertz Library. 2005. "Eleanor Cross Marquand Papers." Finding Aid. The New York Botanical Garden. www.nybg.org/library/finding_guide/archv/marquand_ppf.html.

Ardizzone, Heidi. 2007. *An Illuminated Life: Belle Da Costa Greene's Journey from Prejudice to Privilege*. New York: W. W. Norton.

Arizona Women's Hall of Fame. 2019. "Margaret Bell Douglas (1880–1963)." www.azwhf.org/copy-of-mary-russell-ferrell-colton.

Armstrong, April C. 2019. "Faculty Wives and the Push for Coeducation at Princeton University." Mudd Manuscript Library Blog. November 6. https://blogs.princeton.edu/mudd/2019/11/faculty-wives-and-the-push-for-coeducation-at-princeton-university/.

Ashby, Anna Lou. 2000. "Julia Parker Wightman." In *Grolier 2000: A Further Grolier Club Biographical Retrospective in Celebration of the Millennium*, 391–392. New York: The Grolier Club.

Barlow, Marjorie. 1972. "In Memoriam: Alice Brayton." Box 1. Hroswitha Club Archive at the Grolier Club.

　　1976. *Notes on Women Printers in Colonial America and the United States, 1639–1975*. Charlottesville: University Press of Virginia.

Bartlett, Henrietta C. 1930. "Letter to Belle Da Costa Greene." Box 3, Folder 189. Henrietta C. Bartlett Papers at the Beinecke Library.

　　1935. "Ruth Granniss Celebration Speech." Box 2, Folder 90. Henrietta C. Bartlett Papers at the Beinecke Library.

Bartlett, Henrietta C., and Ruth S. Granniss. 1905. *A Garland of Poppies*. New York: Privately Printed.

Basbanes, Nicholas A. 1999. *A Gentle Madness: Bibliophiles, Bibliomanes, and the Eternal Passion for Books*. New York: Henry Holt and Company.

Baskin, Lisa. 2019. "You Can't Do It Alone." In *The Book Collector*, 10–20. The Collector.

The Morgan Library & Museum. n.d., "Belle Da Costa Greene, the Morgan's First Librarian and Director." Accessed December 28, 2021. www.themorgan.org/belle-greene.

Bibliotheca Phillippica: Catalogue of a Further Portion of the Renowned Library Formed by the Late Sir Thomas Phillipps ... Comprising Autograph Letters and Documents of Great Literary & Historical Importance. 1946. London: Sotheby.

Bigold, Melanie. 2021. "Women's Book Collecting in the Eighteenth Century: The Libraries of the Countess of Hertford and the Duchess of Northumberland." *Huntington Library Quarterly* 84 (1): 139–150.

Bracken, Susan, Andrea M. Gáldy, and Adriana Turpin, eds. 2012. *Women Patrons and Collectors*. Newcastle Upon Tyne: Cambridge Scholars.

Bradley, E. Sculley. 1942. "A Whitman Treasure House." *The University of Pennsylvania Library Chronicle* 10 (2): 27–39.

Bühler, Curt F. 1959. "Howard Lehman Goodhart 1884–1951." In *Grolier 75: A Biographical Retrospective to Celebrate the Seventy-Fifth Anniversary of the Grolier Club in New York*, 218–220. New York: The Grolier Club.

Bull, Katharine [Mrs. Ludlow]. 1964. "Minutes of the Hroswitha Club." Box 1. Hroswitha Club Archive at the Grolier Club.

Chen, Amy Hildreth. 2020. *Placing Papers: The American Literary Archives Market*. Studies in Print Culture and the History of the Book. Amherst: University of Massachusetts Press.

Coleman Jr., Sterling Joseph. 2014. "'Eminently Suited to Girls and Women': The Numerical Feminization of Public Librarianship in England 1914–31." *Libraries & Information History* 30 (3): 195–209.

Cowen, Walker. 1974. "Letter to Mary [Massey]." Box 5. Hroswitha Club Archive at the Grolier Club.

Crenshaw, Kimberlé. 1989. "Demarginalizing the Intersection of Race and Sex: A Black Feminist Critique of Antidiscrimination Doctrine, Feminist Theory and Antiracist Politics." *University of Chicago Legal Forum*, vol 1989, no. 1: 139–167.

Denlinger, Elizabeth C. 2007. "Julia Parker Wightman and the Pierpont Morgan Library." In *Collectors and Collecting: Private Collection and Their Role in Libraries*, 1–12. Hampshire: Chawton House Library.

2008. "Some Women Book Collectors Today." In 1–24. New York.

Dickson, Donald C. 1986. *Dictionary of American Book Collectors*. New York: Greenwood Publishing Group.

Eccles, Mary Hyde. 2002. "Grolier Watching, By a Lady." In *Mary Hyde Eccles: A Miscellany of Her Essays and Addresses*, edited by William Zachs, 249–266. New York: The Grolier Club.

English, Emily [Mrs. Robert B.]. 1948. "Minutes of the Hroswitha Club." Box 2. Hroswitha Club Archive at the Grolier Club.

Farrington, Lynn. 2019. "Collecting Whitman." Case Label presented at the Whitman Vignettes: Camden and Philadelphia, Kislak Center at the University of Pennsylvania.

Fife, Sarah Gildersleeve [Mrs. Robert Herndon]. 1944. "Letter to Mrs. [Catherine Dunscomb] Dickey." Box 2. Hroswitha Club Archive at the Grolier Club.

Folger Shakespeare Library. 1988. *The Grete Herball: Books from the Collection of Mary P. Massey*. Washington, DC: The Folger Shakespeare Library.

Fraser, Robert S. 1972. "The Rossetti Collection of Janet Camp Troxell: A Survey with Some Sidelights." *The Princeton University Library Chronicle* 33 (3): 146–175.

Friedan, Betty. 1963. *The Feminine Mystique*. New York: W. W. Norton.

Gelber, Steven M. 1999. *Hobbies: Leisure and the Culture of Work in America*. New York: Columbia University Press.

Gordan, Phyllis Goodhart. 1955. *Fifteenth-Century Books in the Library of Howard Lehman Goodhart with a Description and Check List*. Stamford, CN: The Overbrook Press. https://repository.brynmawr.edu/bmc_books/28.

Grabhorn, Jane Bissell. 1965. The Colt Press: Oral History Transcript / and Related Material, 1965–196 Interview by Ruth Teiser. BANC MSS C-D 4102. Bancroft Library, University of California Berkeley. https://oac.cdlib.org/search?style=oac4;Institution=UC%20Berkeley::Bancroft%20Library;titlesAZ=C;idT=UCb112349675.

Granniss, Ruth S. 1930. "What Bibliography Owes to Private Book Clubs." *The Papers of the Bibliographical Society of America* 24 (1/2): 14–33.

Greene, Belle Da Costa. 1946. "Letter to Ernst Philip Goldschmidt." Corresp. F-H Mac. PML Records Administration Greene at the Morgan Library & Museum.

Grolier Club. "Hroswitha Club: Records and Publications, 1944–1999." n.d. Finding Aid. www.grolierclub.org/default.aspx?p=v35ListDocument& ID=755370972&listid=11461&listitemid=122614&ssid=322536&dpagei d=&listname=.

Haight, Anne. 1948. "Minutes of the Hroswitha Club." Box 2. Hroswitha Club Archive at the Grolier Club.

　　1949. "Minutes of the Hroswitha Club." Box 1. Hroswitha Club Archive at the Grolier Club.

　　1950. "Minutes of the Hroswitha Club." Box 3. Hroswitha Club Archive at the Grolier Club.

Haight, Anne Lyon. 1946. "Minutes of the Hroswitha Club." Box 2. Hroswitha Club Archive at the Grolier Club.

　　ed. 1965. *Hroswitha of Gandersheim: Her Life, Times, and Works, and a Comprehensive Bibliography*. New York: Hroswitha Club.

Harrsen, Meta. 1960. "Report." In *Minutes of the Hroswitha Club*, by Julia Wightman.

Hastings, Emiko. 2013. "'Mighty Women Book Hunters': A History of American Women Book Collectors." In *Grolier Club*. New York City, New York.

　　2014. "Women Collectors in Their Own Words." *Adventures in Book Collecting* (blog). September 16. https://librarianofbabel.wordpress.com /2014/09/16/women-collectors-in-their-own-words/.

Hendricks, Nancy. 2017. "Women's Club Movement." In Women in American History : A Social, Political, and Cultural Encyclopedia and Document Collection, edited by Peg A. Lamphier and Rosanne Welch, 369–70. Santa Barbara: ABC-CLIO.

Hellman, Geoffrey T. 1959. "Farmington Revisited." *The New Yorker*, October 23. www.newyorker.com/magazine/1959/10/31/farmington-revisited.

Holden, Miriam Y. 1960. *Address to the Hroswitha Club*, Pittsburgh: Privately Printed, 1–15.

Holden, Miriam Young [Mrs. Arthur]. 1960. "Letter to Mrs. [Rachel] Hunt." Holden Collection Box 9, Folder 15. Princeton Rare Books and Manuscripts.

hooks, bell. 1984. *Feminist Theory: From Margin to Center*. Boston: South End Press.

Hooper, Frances. 1973. *Collector in Being*. Kenilworth, IL: The Chihuahua Press.

Horner, Virginia. 1969. "Record Memorandum to Miriam Young Holden." Box 23, Folder 80. Holden Collection at Princeton Rare Books and Manuscripts.

Houghton, Eve 2022. "'I Am Always Sorry to Antagonize Collectors': Henrietta Bartlett and the 1916 Census of Shakespeare Quartos." In *Pantzer New Scholar*. New York. https://youtu.be/5fEqLRjfTpE.

Howell, Hannah. 1973. "In Memoriam: Eleanor Towne Carey." Box 1. Hroswitha Club Archive at the Grolier Club.

Hughey, Matthew W. 2008. "The (Dis)Similarities of White Racial Identities: The Conceptual Framework of 'Hegemonic Whiteness.'" *Ethnic and Racial Studies* 33 (8): 1289–1309.

Hunt Institute for Botanical Documentation. n.d. "Rachel McMasters Miller Hunt." www.huntbotanical.org/about/?4.

Hunt, Rachel [Mrs. Roy A.]. 1960. "Thank You Card." Holden Collection Box 9, Folder 21. Princeton Rare Books and Manuscripts.

John Hay Library. 2018. "Margaret Bingham Stillwell Papers, ca. 1925–1984." Brown University. www.riamco.org/render?eadid=US-RPB-ms-1uf-s3&view=title.

Klemesrud, Judy. 1985. "Her Mission Is Preserving Providence." *The New York Times*, May 2, sec. C.

Lawrence, George H. M., and Miriam Lawrence. 1976. "Letter to Mrs. [Katharine] Peter Oliver." Box 5. Hroswitha Club Archive at the Grolier Club.

Lawrence, Miriam B. 1974. "Minutes of the Hroswitha Club." Hroswitha Club Records at the Grolier Club.

Lawson, Shannon. 1998. "The Press of A. Colish Archives 1913–1990." University of Delaware Library. March. https://library.udel.edu/spe cial/findaids/data/pdf/mss0358.pdf.

Leazes, Francis J., and J. Joseph Garrahy. 2004. *Providence, The Renaissance City*. Boston: Northeastern University Press.

Lerner, Gerda. 1980. "Miriam Holden–In Remembrance and Friendship." *The Princeton University Library Chronicle* 41 (2): 164–168.

Lesser, Zachary, and Eve Houghton. 2020. "Recovering Henrietta Bartlett, Shakespeare Bibliographer." Beinecke Rare Book & Manuscript Library. April 23. https://beinecke.library.yale.edu/article/zachary-lesser-and-eve-houghton-recovering-henrietta-bartlett-shakespeare-bibliographer.

Long, Elizabeth. 2003. *Book Clubs: Women and the Uses of Reading in Everyday Life*. Chicago: University of Chicago Press.

Lorde, Audre. 1984. "Age, Race, Class and Sex: Women Redefining Difference." In *Sister Outsider: Essays and Speeches by Audre Lorde*, 110–123. Berkeley: Crossing Press.

Macleod, Dianne Sachko. 2008. *Enchanted Lives, Enchanted Objects: American Women Collectors and the Making of Culture, 1800–1940*. Berkeley: University of California Press.

Markham, Sandra. 2018. "Guide to the Annie Burr Lewis Papers." Finding Aid. Lewis Walpole Library at Yale University. http://hdl.handle.net/10079/fa/lwl.mss.021.

Matthews, Jack. 1977. *Collecting Rare Books for Pleasure and Profit*. New York: G. P. Putnam's Sons.

Maybanks, Sheila. 1970. "Letter to Marjorie Barlow." Box 5. Hroswitha Club Archive at the Grolier Club.

Morgan, Sarah [Mrs. Charles]. 2003. "Memo from Sarah Morgan." Box 2. Hroswitha Club Archive at the Grolier Club.

Morris, Jerry. 2008. "Mary Hyde and the Unending Pursuit." *Bibliophiles in My Library* (blog). November 6. https://bibliophilesinmylibrary.blogspot.com/2008/11/mary-hyde-and-unending-pursuit.html.

Ong, George, and Eric J. Holzenberg. 2009. "Fifteenth Century Books and the Twentieth Century. An Address by Curt F. Bühler, and a Catalogue of an Exhibition of Fifteenth Century Books Held at The Grolier Club, April 15-June 1, 1952." In *For Jean Grolier & His Friends: 125 Years of Grolier Club Exhibitions and Publications 1884–2009*, 356–357. New York: The Grolier Club.

Orseman, Donald. 2004. "Letter to Susannah [Mrs. Livio] Borghese." Box 2. Hroswitha Club Archive at the Grolier Club.

Ozment, Kate. 2020. "Rationale for Feminist Bibliography." *Textual Cultures* 13 (1): 1–30. https://doi.org/10.14434/textual.v13i1.30076.

Pearce, Susan. 1995. *On Collecting: An Investigation into Collecting in the European Tradition*. New York: Routledge.

Phipps, Frances. 1981. "Antiques; Prescott Collection Surprises Auctioneer." *The New York Times*, March 1, www.nytimes.com/1981/03/01/nyregion/antiques-prescott-collection-surprises-auctioneer.html.

Pollak, Benjamin H. 2021. "'A New Ethnology': The Legal Expansion of Whiteness under Early Jim Crow." *Law and History Review* 39 (3): 513–538. https://doi.org/10.1017/S0738248021000110.

Prescott, Marjorie Wiggin. 1932. *Stray Thoughts of a Book Collector*. New York: Privately Printed.

President and Fellows of Yale University. 1947. "Letter to Mr. and Mrs. Donald F. Hyde." April 19. Yale University Correspondence, 1947–1983. Mary Hyde Eccles Papers at the Houghton Library.

Princeton University Library. 2020. "Coeducation: History of Women at Princeton University." August 26. https://libguides.princeton.edu/coed.

Providence Preservation Society. n.d. "Who We Are." About. Accessed January 18, 2022. https://ppsri.org/about/.

Quinby, Jane, and Barlow, Marjorie. 1960. "Miss Jane Quinby's Report on Progress to Mrs. Barlow." In *Minutes of the Hroswitha Club*, by Julia P. Wightman.

Rather, Lois. 1970. "Letter to Marjorie Barlow." Box 5. Hroswitha Club Archive at the Grolier Club.

    1974. "Letter to Marjorie Barlow." Box 5. Hroswitha Club Archive at the Grolier Club.

    1975. "Letter to Marjorie Barlow." Box 5. Hroswitha Club Archive at the Grolier Club.

Rich, Adrienne. 1980. "Compulsory Heterosexuality and Lesbian Existence." *Signs* 5 (4): 631–660.

Riley, Elizabeth. 1984. "In Memoriam." Box 1. Hroswitha Club Archive at the Grolier Club.

Riley, Elizabeth M. [Mrs. Charles F.]. 2001. "Letter to Sally Morgan." Box 2. Hroswitha Club Archive at the Grolier Club.

Rosenbach, A. S. W. 1927. "Why America Buys England's Books." In *Books and Bidders: The Adventures of a Bibliophile with Illustrations*, 243–263. Boston: Little, Brown.

    1936. "Mighty Women Book Hunters." In *A Book Hunter's Holiday: Adventures with Books and Manuscripts*, 105–130. Boston: Houghton Mifflin.

Rosenblum, Joseph. 1997. *American Book-Collectors and Bibliographers*. Dictionary of Literary Biography 187. Detroit: Bruccoli Clark Layman and Gale Research.

Ryskamp, Charles. 1969. "Hroswitha at Princeton." *The Princeton University Library Chronicle* 30 (2): 123–126.

Scheil, Katherine West. 2012. *She Hath Been Reading: Women and Shakespeare Clubs in America*. Ithaca: Cornell University Press.

Sedgwick, Eve Kosofsky. 1985. *Between Men: English Literature and Male Homosocial Desire*. New York: Columbia University Press.

Slack, Nancy G. 1989. "Nineteenth-Century American Women Botanists: Wives, Widows, and Work." In *Uneasy Careers and Intimate Lives: Women in Science, 1789–1979*, edited by Margaret W. Rossiter, 77–103. New Brunswick: Rutgers University Press.

Smith, Leslie. 2018. "Walt Whitman Collections." Finding Aid. Kislak Center at the University of Pennsylvania. http://dla.library.upenn.edu/dla/pacscl/ead.pdf?id=PACSCL_UPENN_RBML_MsColl190.

Special Collections Department Staff. n.d. "A Guide to the Linton Massey Papers Relating to the William Faulkner Collection and the William Faulkner Foundation, 1953–1974." Finding Aid. University of Virginia Library, Special Collections, Alderman Library. https://ead.lib.virginia.edu/vivaxtf/view?docId=uva-sc/viu01168.xml;query=;brand=default.

Sprague, Harriet Chapman [Mrs. Frank Julian]. 1939. *A List of Manuscripts, Books, Portraits, Prints, Broadsides and Memorabilia in Commemoration of the One Hundred and Twentieth Anniversary of the Birth of Walt Whitman from the Whitman Collection of Mrs. Frank Julian Sprague of New York City, Exhibited at the Library of Congress, 1939*. Washington, DC: Government Print Office.

Stammers, Tom. 2021. "Women Collectors and Cultural Philanthropy, c. 1850–1920." *19: Interdisciplinary Studies in the Long Nineteenth Century*, no. 31. https://doi.org/10.16995/ntn.3347.

Stewart, Seumas. 1973. *Book Collecting: A Beginner's Guide*. New York: E. P. Dutton.

Stillwell, Margaret Bingham. 1940. *The Annmary Brown Memorial; a Booklover's Shrine*. Providence, RI: Privately Printed.

1943. *While Benefit Street Was Young*. Providence: The Ackerman-Standard Press.

1945. *The Pageant of Benefit Street: Down through the Years*. Providence: The Ackerman-Standard Press.

Tamarkin, Elisa. 2008. *Anglophilia: Deference, Devotion, and Antebellum America*. Chicago: The University of Chicago Press.

Tanselle, G. Thomas. 1977. "The Literature of Book Collecting." In *Book Collecting: A Modern Guide*, edited by Jean Peters, 209–272. New York: R. R. Bowker.

Taylor, Julia. 1995. "Left on the Shelf? The Issues and Challenges Facing Women Employed in Libraries from the Late Nineteenth Century to the 1950s." *Library History* 11 (1): 96–107.

Taylor, Keeanga-Yamahtta. 2012. *How We Get Free: Black Feminism and the Combahee River Collective*. Chicago: Haymarket Books.

Teltsch, Kathleen. 1968. "Volunteers Give Freely of Their Time to Aid City and Charities." *The New York Times*, March 31, 117 ed. www.nytimes.com/1968/03/31/archives/volunteers-give-freely-of-their-time-to-aid-city-and-charities.html.

Terry, Miss [Theresa]. 1969. "Letter to Marjorie Barlow." Box 5. Hroswitha Club Archive at the Grolier Club.

The Grolier Club. 1976. "Letter to Mrs. Donald Hyde." September 27. Grolier Club, 1960–2003 and undated. Mary Hyde Eccles Papers at the Houghton Library.

The Hartford Courant. 2000. "Swaim, Elizabeth Ann." May 17, sec. Obituaries. www.courant.com/news/connecticut/hc-xpm-2000-05-17-0005161859-story.html.

The New York Times. 1979. "Wilmarth S. Lewis, 83, Horace Walpole Expert." October 8, 129 ed., sec. B. www.nytimes.com/1979/10/08/archives/wilmarth-s-lewis-83-horace-walpole-expert.html.

————. 1983. "Elizabeth Frelinghuysen Dies; Active in Historical Societies." April 30, 132 ed., sec. 1.

The New Yorker. 1957. "Hroswithians." Holden Collection Box 63, Folder 30. Princeton Rare Books and Manuscripts.

Tóth, Heléna. 2003. "Building 'Wisdom and Stability': Mary Lowell Putnam's Library and Women's Book Culture in the Nineteenth Century." *Harvard Library Bulletin*, New Series, 14 (3): 33–48.

Troxell, Gilbert McCoy. 1933. "The Elizabethan Club of Yale University." *Papers of the Bibliographical Society of America* 27: 83–88.

Tuckerman, Jane G. 1976. "Letter to Marjorie Barlow." Box 5. Hroswitha Club Archive at the Grolier Club.

Unknown. 1967. *Untitled Photograph*. Photograph. BMS Hyde 98. Mary Hyde Eccles Papers at the Houghton Library.

————. 1968. "Minutes of the Hroswitha Club." Box 1. Hroswitha Club Archive at the Grolier Club.

————. 2004. "Transcription of Grolier Council Meeting Minutes." Box 2. Hroswitha Club Archive at the Grolier Club.

————. 2005. "Membership List." Box 2. Hroswitha Club Archive at the Grolier Club.

Walker, Susan. 2021. "Doing Good by Stealth: The Philanthropy and Service of Annie Burr Lewis." Yale University Library Online Exhibitions. March 2021. https://onlineexhibits.library.yale.edu/s/doing-good-by-stealth/page/tributes.

Walkup, Kathleen. 2011. "Printing at the Margins: An Ink-Stained History of Women & Work." In San Francisco Public Library. www .youtube.com/watch?v=aiphuOw6ISQ&ab_channel=SanFrancisco PublicLibrary.

Ward, Gordon. 1947. "King Wihtred's Charter of AD 699." *Archaeologia Cantiana* 60: 1–14.

West Newbury Riding Driving Club. 2016. "Remembering Deirdre H Pirie." Facebook. February 4, 2016. www.facebook.com/145918648793428/ photos/remembering-deirdre-h-pirieon-january-17th-deidre-h-pirie-of-hamilton-ma-an-extr/1106072766111340/.

Wightman, Julia P. 1961. "Minutes of the Hroswitha Club." Box 1. Hroswitha Club Archive at the Grolier Club.

    1963a. "Minutes of the Hroswitha Club." Box 1. Hroswitha Club Archive at the Grolier Club.

    1963b. "Minutes of the Hroswitha Club." Box 1. Hroswitha Club Archive at the Grolier Club.

    1988. "Hroswitha Club Meeting." Box 2. Hroswitha Club Archive at the Grolier Club.

    1990. "Hroswitha Club Meeting." Box 2. Hroswitha Club Archive at the Grolier Club.

Wilson, Robert A. 1980. *Modern Book Collecting*. New York: Alfred A. Knopf.

Winterich, John T., and David A. Randall. 1966. *A Primer of Book Collecting*. 3rd revised ed. New York: Crown.

Wong, Kelly. 2020. "The Collector's Role in the Canon." In Student Research, Scholarship & Creative Activities Conference, California State Polytechnic University, Pomona: ScholarWorks. http://hdl .handle.net/20.500.12680/h415pf452.

Woolf, Virginia. 2005. *A Room of One's Own*. Annotated by Susan Gubar. New York: Harcourt, Inc.

Young, Marian W. 1982. "In Memoriam." Box 1. Hroswitha Club Archive at the Grolier Club.

Acknowledgments

My thanks to those who have helped shape this Element through draft feedback: Meghan Constantinou, Michelle Levy, Samantha Rayner, my two peer reviewers, and the audience at the UCLA event on feminist bibliographies.

Cambridge Elements ≡

Publishing and Book Culture

SERIES EDITOR
Samantha Rayner
University College London

Samantha Rayner is Professor of Publishing and Book
Cultures at UCL. She is also Director of UCL's Centre for
Publishing, co-Director of the Bloomsbury CHAPTER
(Communication History, Authorship, Publishing, Textual
Editing and Reading) and co-Chair of the Bookselling
Research Network.

ASSOCIATE EDITOR
Leah Tether
University of Bristol

Leah Tether is Professor of Medieval Literature and
Publishing at the University of Bristol. With an academic
background in medieval French and English literature and
a professional background in trade publishing, Leah has
combined her expertise and developed an international
research profile in book and publishing history from
manuscript to digital.

About the Series

This series aims to fill the demand for easily accessible, quality texts
available for teaching and research in the diverse and dynamic fields
of Publishing and Book Culture. Rigorously researched and peer-
reviewed Elements will be published under themes, or "Gatherings".
These Elements should be the first check point for researchers or
students working on that area of publishing and book trade history
and practice: we hope that, situated so logically at Cambridge
University Press, where academic publishing in the UK began, it will
develop to create an unrivalled space where these histories and
practices can be investigated and preserved.

Cambridge Elements ≡

Publishing and Book Culture

Collecting the Book

Gathering Editor: Cynthia Johnston

Cynthia Johnston is a Lecturer in the History of the Book and
Communication at the Institute of English Studies, School of
Advanced Study, University of London where she directs the
MA programme in the History of the Book. Her research
interests focus on the history of book collecting and book
cultures.

ELEMENTS IN THE GATHERING

A full series listing is available at: www.cambridge.org/EPBC

Printed in the United States
by Baker & Taylor Publisher Services